Accessing Your Prophetic Gift

BARBARA WENTROBLE

FOREWORD

I have known Prophet Barbara Wentroble for many years. We have been co-speakers in many conferences, prophetic councils and meetings. Barbara functions similar as I do—a prophet to the Body of Christ but an apostle to her own.

I have to know a person's life in the 10 M's and their wisdom and balance in presenting the prophetic in their teaching and ministry before putting my name and endorsement to the book. Barbara Wentroble definitely meets all of these standards.

In 1988 the prophetic movement was birthed at a Christian International conference. I received a heavenly vision and commissioning from Christ to take a fathering role in co-laboring with Jesus to raise up the prophets and prophetic in wisdom and integrity while maintaining and maturing the anointing and ministry. It is important for Christians to understand God's many reasons for bringing about the restoration of prophets and prophetic ministry back into His Church.

Thank you, Barbara, for taking time to write your books on prophets and the prophetic. They are so necessary. Your books are enlightening and motivational. Myself being a Church historian on Church restoration movements, I know from history and experience that if books are not written immediately after a restoration movement takes place, then the truths and ministries are not properly established in the Church. That's the reason I wrote the trilogy of books including *Prophets and Personal Prophecy*, *Prophets and the Prophetic Movement* and *Prophetic Pitfalls to Avoid and Principles to Practice*.

Now, Barbara, 30 years later after all your years of prophetic ministry as an apostolic prophet, you are writing books that will enable this present generation to fulfill their call to be sons and daughters of God who can prophesy with wisdom, anointing and integrity. Anyone who reads this book with an open mind and a hungry heart will be educated, motivated and activated into God's prophetic lifestyle and ministry.

Barbara, you bless my 84-year-old prophetic, father heart to see such quality prophetic material going out to Christ's Church. Bless you, Barbara, and keep producing books and raising up God's prophetic army for these last days.

Bishop Bill Hamon
Christian International Apostolic-Global Network

Author: *The Eternal Church, Prophets & Personal Prophecy, Prophets & the Prophetic Movement, Prophets, Pitfalls, & Principles, Apostles/Prophets & the Coming Moves of God, The Day of the Saints, Who Am I & Why Am I Here, Prophetic Scriptures Yet to be Fulfilled (3rd Reformation), 70 Reasons for Speaking in Tongues, and How Can These Things Be? God's World War III*

INTRODUCTION

More than 100,000 people were told to evacuate! The area had experienced several years of drought. However, recent rains were causing the dam's spillway to be in danger of breaking. If the break occurred, the flood water would endanger the lives of those in its path. Frantic efforts were being carried out to repair the spillway.

I listened to the news report. My heart was touched, and I prayed for those in that area. I couldn't imagine all they were going through to find a safe place and leave their homes and possessions behind. The prospects of a destructive river flooding their area was a real threat.

At the same time, I was praying for those people, I was reminded of a refreshing prophetic river that the Lord is ready to release on Earth. This prophetic river will spill out into the dry, barren places on Earth. This river is able to touch lives that have never been touched before. The Lord is ready to release His prophetic river in the Earth's desert places.

> Do not call to mind the former things, or ponder things of the past. Behold, I will do something new, now it will spring forth; Will you not be aware of it? I will even make a roadway in the wilderness, rivers in the desert.
>
> Isaiah 43:18–19

Past moves of God experienced powerful demonstrations of the Spirit. Past revelation was impressive in its day. We are thankful for those moves and appreciate what God did in the past. Yet, we cannot live in the past. God has opened the realm of the Spirit and is revealing new things to this generation. Today, God is releasing revelation in proportions that were unheard of in the past.

Life in the Spirit is like the upgrading of computers. We are in our *kairos* time to jump into the prophetic river that God is releasing in this season. A kairos time is an opportune time. It is a time when the Lord is ready to do something new. God wants to upgrade us in fresh, new revelation, prophetic gifts and our impact on Earth. He will do this as we access our prophetic gift from the Council Room of the Lord!

We are like Jacob in our wrestling to get into God's new prophetic move of the Spirit. The old religious order is struggling to stay alive. The traditional religious order denies that speaking in tongues is for today. It denies that prophets and prophecy are for today. The religious leaders believe prophetic people are merely troublemakers. The Early Church experienced the effect of what they considered troublemakers. That Church was so full of the Holy Spirit that they seemed to constantly cause trouble with the old religious order.

To stay alive, this old religious order is gasping for breath. The new prophetic move of God is in the birth pangs of bringing forth a new prophetic move! Prophets and prophetic people are about to birth something new on Earth. Like the dam ready to break, like the waters in a woman about to give birth… the waters of a new prophetic move are pressing to break open.

> Jacob was left alone, and a man wrestled with him until daybreak. When he saw that he had not prevailed against him, he

> touched the socket of his thigh; so the socket of Jacob's thigh was dislocated while he wrestled with him. Then he said, "Let me go, for the dawn is breaking." But he said, "I will not let you go unless you bless me." So he said to him, "What is your name?" And he said, "Jacob." And he said, "Your name shall no longer be Jacob, but Israel; for you have striven with God and with men and have prevailed."
>
> Genesis 32:24–28

God wrestled with Jacob. Today, God is wrestling to bring His people into their true prophetic identity. Your past identity is not who you are. It is not your potential nor your future. You have access to your prophetic gift from God's Council Room. Your access will unlock your new prophetic identity. Like Jacob of old, you are ready for a name change. Jacob became Israel. Israel means "striver with God." It also means "God commands." Jacob wrestled until the daybreak.

You are standing at the end of the darkness of your night season. You are entering the daybreak of a new beginning in your prophetic destiny. You are wrestling to break out of your old identity. You are hearing the command of the Lord to step into His Council Room. Agree with Him that you will not leave until you access your prophetic gift!

Jacob's time had come for transformation in his life so that he could apprehend his prophetic destiny. God has an opportune timing for releasing your prophetic destiny. A kairos moment in your life will connect Heaven to Earth. It unlocks what is in Heaven and brings it to Earth. Your kairos prophetic moment will release you into God's prophetic purpose for your life. Like Jacob of old, we are wrestling to break into this fresh prophetic river.

God's prophetic voice was used in Genesis 1 to bring order out of the chaos and disorder. He called into being what had never been created. The prophetic voice creates what has never been created in the past. What was chaos, now had become peaceful. The prophetic voice brings peace during the day's turmoil. What was in confusion became clear and in order. What was dark and hidden became light and visible. Prophetic revelation will bring clarity and reveal hidden mysteries of the past.

God reaches out and captures a willing prophetic voice. This voice speaks to a broken and battered world. God's prophetic voice speaks to a cause greater than the messenger. Prophets are not speaking in their own strength but by the power of the Holy Spirit. Out of the person's own transformation, they become a prophetic river to release a decree. The decree breaks the chains of death. The prophetic voice identifies with the pain and suffering of others. The prophetic voice hates injustice. It brings light and hope to a dark world.

Nabi is one of the Hebrew words for *prophet*. This word gives a picture of a boiling forth, a gushing out, a flowing forth like a fountain or a gushing river. The power of Holy Spirit is so big inside it must gush forth like a river to a broken, chaotic world.

> He who believes in Me, as the Scripture said, "From his innermost being shall flow rivers of living water."
>
> John 7:38

This prophetic river must be released to break chains from the captives.

> Again he measured a thousand; and it was
> a river that I could not ford, for the water
> had risen, enough water to swim in, a river
> that could not be forded.
>
> Ezekiel 47:5

The prophetic river of God is rising. It is a river that is too deep to wade through. Only the Lord can hold you up in this river. Yet, He is faithful. He walked you through waters in the past. He protected you through the storms. None of that was strong enough to destroy you. Now you face a new challenge. Can you trust the Lord who brought you through the storms and floods of the past to bring you to a new level in God's prophetic river today?

You are probably reading this book because you are hungry for a fresh prophetic move of God's Spirit. My desire is that you will embrace the fullness of your spiritual inheritance. Step into the daybreak of your future. Volunteer freely in the day of God's prophetic power (Psalm 110:3). Your prophetic gift is powerful enough to heal bodies, emotions, cities and territories. Access your prophetic gift from the Council Room of the Lord and let the river flow!

DEDICATION

Dedicated to Chuck Pierce, a modern-day Issachar prophet of God, a great encourager, a co-laborer in ministry and a friend to our family. His powerful prophetic ministry and sensitive spirit has made an impact around the world.

When Chuck and I were first introduced, the prayer movement was just beginning to gain momentum. Through the years as the movement matured, one of the powerful outcomes was an awakening of the prophetic spirit. Ordinary believers had the infilling of the Holy Spirit and began to experience hearing the voice of the Lord. The phenomenon resulted in the Charismatic Movement that spread the gifts of the Holy Spirit around the globe.

I have had the pleasure and joy of watching the prophetic spirit become established throughout the world. Today, Chuck Pierce is one of the most well-known and respected prophetic voices globally. His life is a validation of God raising up powerful prophets to speak to today's world.

BARBARA WENTROBLE

CONTENTS

BARBARA WENTROBLE

CHAPTER 1

Called to Prophesy

The road trip to the retreat was exciting! We talked nonstop about seeing friends, enjoying food without our cooking and cleaning up and time to focus on what the Lord had for our future. My friend, Kim, drove the car as we discussed our understanding of the calling from the Lord. By that time, I had seen the Lord perform amazing miracles of healing. I witnessed his deliverance in people who were tormented in their minds. I was convinced that He is a God of might and power. Yet, there was one gift that did not seem to apply to my life.

"One thing I know," I remarked. "I am not a prophet and not called to prophetic ministry." I was comfortable with seeing people healed and set free. People love you when you allow the Lord to use you to release healing and deliverance. They are not always happy when you speak a word to them that does not meet their expectations. Maybe that was the reason I was not open to the idea of being used in prophetic ministry.

Immediately, Kim pulled the car over to the side of the road and stopped the car. She looked at my face and with great conviction said, "You need to go back and think about that again!" I trusted her spiritual insight but was shaken by what she said.

"Is it possible that I have missed what God has for my life?" I thought.

"Have I been resisting God's call due to the desire to remain in a comfortable place?"

"Is there a gift inside me that I have failed to recognize?"

The admonition from my friend caused me to rethink God's plan for my life. I remembered growing up in an evangelical church. We were told that there are no prophets today. The doctrine is known as *cessationism.* This belief teaches that prophecy and other spiritual gifts stopped functioning when the New Testament was completed.

Yet, as I read the Bible, I discovered many scriptures that validated God's plan for prophecy and spiritual gifts to be accessed by all Christians.

> For you can all prophesy one by one, so that all may learn, and all may be exhorted.
>
> 1 Corinthians 14:31

Reading that scripture reminded me that the Lord made prophecy available to every believer. If I am a believer, I should be operating in prophecy. My challenge was to change my mind. Suddenly, I realized I needed to *desire* to prophesy! "Therefore, my brethren desire earnestly to prophesy" (1 Corinthians 14:39).

As I meditated on God's plan for believers to operate in prophecy, I remembered times in my childhood. Often, I would "know" some things that I did not know in the natural. I remembered having dreams or visions about situations where I did not have understanding. Through the years, I met many people who shared similar situations in their lives. They experienced dreams, visions and a knowing about situations, from the time they were children. These people did not understand that the Lord had a prophetic gift in them from birth. Often, this gift has been dormant and not embraced. People around them did not know about the power of dreams and visions. How sad that they had not experienced the joy of releasing this prophetic gift.

Our granddaughter, Gabi, often has prophetic dreams and visions. People were amazed as she boldly stood before a large congregation while numerous nations were watching by webcast.

Ten-year-old Gabriella Kooiman released the following vision: "I saw a man sitting on church steps. He was poor and older, and he had a basket with a sign that said, 'Please give me food or money.' He put his head down and closed his eyes, and when he opened them up he saw kids of age 5 to 12 coming down the church steps with food, water and money. The kids were dumping them into his basket."

Chuck Pierce spoke and released the prophetic interpretation of the vision.

> I am connecting generations! Where one generation didn't have the provision, they needed to accomplish their call, I'll send another generation to unlock and pour in so that what needs to be finished in one generation will now be finished in another generation. I am an abundant God, and I am a Father who is capable of giving what

> I need to give. I am now unlocking what
> you need to finish strong! I am connecting
> the generations. I am moving in ways you
> can't understand. I am a good Father.

The Bible recounts the story of a child named Samuel. The prophetic word of God was rare in those days. The religious order included the sons of the priest, Eli. Regrettably, they had corrupted and tarnished the priesthood. Into this deplorable situation was born a baby to a desperate couple. The baby, Samuel, was dedicated to the Lord at an early age. He was presented to Eli as a gift to the Lord. Samuel was a "first fruit" prophet that would later raise up a company of prophets. He is often thought of as the "first of the prophets."[1] His gift was destined to multiply beyond his own lifetime.

In the midst of the defiled religious system, young Samuel learned to hear the prophetic word of the Lord. During a night when Samuel was in bed, he heard a voice calling his name. Thinking it was Eli, young Samuel ran to him. Eli sent Samuel back to bed, letting him know that he had not called him. After the same incident happened a couple times, Eli knew that the young boy was hearing the Lord. He sent Samuel back to bed to listen to the Lord. Samuel was prepared to hear what God was speaking. "The Lord came and stood and called as at other times, 'Samuel! Samuel!' And Samuel said, 'Speak for Thy servant is listening'" (1 Samuel 3:10).

Young Samuel did not recognize the voice of the Lord at that early age. He was learning to discern the voice of God. God's prophetic purpose for Samuel

---

[1] Ernest B. Gentile, *Your Sons and Daughters Shall Prophesy* (Grand Rapids, Michigan: Chosen, 1999), 85.

manifested as a child and would eventually propel him into his destiny as a prophet. Often, God's training for His prophetic people begins during childhood.

Years ago, Dale and I were pastors of a local church. We were developing home groups as places of training and discipleship. One night I helped with the children at a home meeting. I told the story of young Samuel to the children. It was explained that like Samuel, they could hear the voice of the Lord. After a time of prayer, the children were asked to listen for the Lord to speak to them. I wrote down the messages that the children felt God spoke to them. I was amazed at the depth and clarity of the messages.

Later that evening, I shared with the parents. "Would you like to hear what your children prophesied in the other room?" I asked. The look on the faces of the parents as I read the messages was one of shock! Most of them did not prophesy. They were filled with amazement that their children could hear the prophetic word of the Lord so clearly. I believe in provoking people to good things. I think that I provoked the parents to get busy growing in their spiritual gift of prophecy, so they could keep up with their kids!

Not everyone has the privilege of learning to hear the voice of the Lord at a young age. However, all believers can learn to discern the voice of the Lord. Every believer is able to stand in the Council of the Lord and hear the word of the Lord.

> Who has stood in the council of the Lord,
> that he should see and hear His word?
> > Jeremiah 23:18

God's word in His Council Room often confirms His call

on a person's life. You become passionate to live a life of significance.

Moses was a prophet that God called from His Council Room. A Hebrew, he grew up under the Pharaoh System. That system had Pharaoh positioned as the highest authority. Under Pharaoh was God. People could worship God but only in isolation. They could worship God in homes and buildings but not in public. The Pharaoh System determines what is right and what is wrong. When God is positioned as the highest authority, people are free to worship wherever they are.

Regardless of the system Moses grew up in, he knew from an early age that he was called to be a deliverer of God's people. His natural mother, Jochebed, was able to raise him for the first few months of his life. Jochebed was a daughter of Levi and mother of Aaron, Miriam and Moses. I believe she made a deposit of God in her baby that would remain throughout his life. Although he was taken from her and spent his growing up years in the palace of Pharaoh, he never lost the spiritual deposit made by Jochebed. The time came when Moses remembered that he was a Hebrew and not an Egyptian. The spiritual deposit put within him as a baby surfaced. It was not lost! That should bring hope to many parents and grandparents who see their children living in undesirable situations!

Moses attempted at one point to step into God's call. He killed an Egyptian in the pursuit of his calling. Afterwards, he spent 40 years on the backside of the desert. Moses may have questioned his call from God during those years. Prophets and prophetic people go through difficult seasons in life.

A shift in the life of Moses occurred as he was pasturing the flock of his father-in-law, Jethro. The angel of the Lord appeared to him in a blazing fire from Heaven. Moses turned aside to see the bush that was burning and yet was not consumed. His curiosity led him to the entrance of the Council Room of the Lord. God's Council Room can manifest in some of the most unusual places, even in the midst of smelly sheep!

God would now confirm the call on Moses' life from His Council Room. He made sure that Moses knew God's call had not been revoked due to earlier situations. Sometimes people think that their past has negated the call of God for their lives. Failures, sin, disobedience and all sorts of excuses attempt to get people to discard their calling from the Lord. Moses needed to know that his past was not his potential. God still had a call on his life! "The gifts and calling of God are irrevocable" (Romans 11:29).

The shift in Moses' life caused a prophetic shift on Earth. The prophetic word from the Lord to Moses would bring about the deliverance of a nation. The Council Room of the Lord is a "War Room." Strategies to win earthly battles are settled in this War Room. Strategies are released to break the powers of torment, fears, injustice, infirmity, corruption and many other evil powers. These evil forces are dismantled through decisions from the Council Room.

> God has taken his place in the divine council; in the midst of the gods he holds judgement.
>
> Psalm 82:1 ESV

God was issuing a call to a man who would dialogue with Him in His Council Room. Moses would need to know that he was God's prophet, and it was God who was sending him to deliver God's people.

> When the Lord saw that he turned aside
> to look, God called to him from the midst
> of the bush, and said, "Moses, Moses!"
> and he said, "Here I am."
>
> Exodus 3:4

At this encounter, Moses and God dialogued about Moses' assignment in Egypt. They discussed how Moses would confront Pharaoh. They talked about the supernatural power God would release through Moses to convince Pharaoh to let God's people go from their captivity. God did not reprimand Moses for questioning Him. Discussion, deliberations and questions are acceptable protocol in God's Council Room. Prophets and prophetic people must know who they are and who sent them.

God assured Moses of his identity as God's prophet and His sending to and His sending by God to fulfill the heart of God for His people.

> Moses said to God, "Who am I, that I
> should go to Pharaoh, and that I should
> bring the sons of Israel out of Egypt?"
> God said to Moses, "I AM WHO I AM";
> and He said, "Thus you shall say to the
> sons of Israel, 'I AM has sent me to you'"
>
> Exodus 3:11, 14

Knowing God's call for his life helped Moses be successful in the prophetic assignment God had for him on Earth. Believers today need to know God's call on their lives, so they can be successful in the assignment they have on Earth. God will confirm His prophetic call on your life in many ways.

Just like Moses and many other biblical leaders, you and I are called to be the voice of the Lord and inspire His people to know God's calling.

God may confirm His call through a prophetic word. The Apostle Paul encouraged young Timothy to fight through difficulties by remembering his call that came through a prophetic utterance. "This command I entrust to you, Timothy, my son, in accordance with the prophecies previously made concerning you, that by them you may fight the good fight" (1 Timothy 1:18). There will be days when it seems that maybe God didn't really call you. The prophetic word is a weapon in your prophetic arsenal to help you win the battle!

The Bible tells the story of Joseph and his prophetic call through a dream. One of the meanings of Joseph's name is "Revealer of Secrets."[2] Joseph would reveal secrets in hearts of people, even though he was in prison, in Potiphar's house or wherever he was. No matter the situation he interpreted dreams, but he also revealed secret conditions in the hearts of people. Joseph dreamed about his future when he was 17 years old. He saw his family bowing down before him. "For behold, we were binding sheaves in the field, and lo, my sheaf rose up and also stood erect; and behold, your sheaves gathered around and bowed down to my sheaf" (Genesis 37:7). God opened His Council Room for Joseph to see his prophetic destiny. Frequently, God reveals destinies through dreams and visions.

Prophets and prophetic people are called to be God's deliverers today. The call is not limited to the

---

[2] Arthur Pink, *Gleanings in Genesis* (Chicago, IL: Moody Press, 1950), 344.

spiritually elite, people with religious titles or people with the largest ministries. The call to the Council Room is for all believers.

The platform for your call is your ability to influence the lives of others. Keep moving forward and see the Lord bring you into your divine purpose.

As a believer, you are part of the royal priesthood that Jesus purchased through His death on the Cross.

> But you are A CHOSEN RACE, A royal PRIESTHOOD, A HOLY NATION, A PEOPLE for God's own POSSESSION, that you may proclaim the excellencies of Him who has called you out of darkness into His marvelous light.
>
> 1 Peter 2:9

> Raised us up with Him, and seated us with Him in the heavenly places, in Christ Jesus.
>
> Ephesians 2:6

Times have changed. A shift has occurred! The new generation of a prophetic priesthood is arising. They have conversed with the King of Glory in His Council Room. They are called to deliver Earth into a heavenly pattern. They know who they are and Who is sending them to release the will of God into Earth. You have a call to be part of this prophetic priesthood. Will you answer God's call and enter His Council Room?

Practical Steps

1. Describe a time when you knew something that you did not know in the natural.

2. What is a mindset that needs to change for you to embrace your call?

3. Explain a dream or vision that you experienced and did not understand. What did you do to bring clarity?

4. Talk about a time when you sensed the Lord calling you to do something that you were hesitant to do. Why were you hesitant?

5. What situation or people group do you feel called to deliver from evil powers?

CHAPTER 2

Accessing Your Prophetic Mantle

I was standing by my seat on the front row as the speaker ministered a corporate prophetic word to the attendees at the conference. I don't remember what the word was. I just knew that as he was speaking, I suddenly stepped into God's Council Room. (See my book, *Accessing the Power of God.*) Everything else that was happening around me was out of my physical hearing and awareness.

My hands were raised to the Lord. Suddenly, I felt a powerful thrust as I sensed something coming into my hands. The thrust was so strong that I stumbled backwards toward my chair. My spiritual eyes were immediately opened, and I had a vision. Crossways in my hands was a long sword. I knew the sword was from the Lord but was not fully aware of what that meant.

A couple years later, I was speaking at another conference. At the end of the conference, the pastor and several leaders gathered around me to pray. While they were praying, I again had a vision of the sword laying crossways in my hands. Once again, the power of the sword was heavy and caused a thrust as it came into my hands. However, this time I saw the sword lift and point vertically after it came into my hands.

After the prayer time, I met with a couple pastors in the church office. I explained the two visions with the swords. I knew God was doing something but didn't understand the impact of what happened in both of those instances. One pastor interpreted the visions and powerful thrust of the swords. He said the cross-ward sword was a Prophetic Gathering authority. I was mantled to gather God's prophetic people. The people would gather to be trained, activated and equipped for their prophetic call. He said that in the second vison, when the sword went up, that was a Prophetic Advancing authority. Prophetic people would be mantled, commissioned and sent to release God's will into Earth.

New Mantles of Authority

Later, I understood that these visions of the sword were pictures of new mantles of authority that were released upon me.

Mantles from the Lord are designed to empower people with spiritual authority to function at a higher level than they could in the past. Prophets and prophetic people fight fierce battles. They go into enemy territory to extend the rule of Jesus in those places. They need a higher level of spiritual authority to bring the will of God into Earth.

Higher levels of authority always sound exciting. We think about the new adventures coming our way. It is like looking at a beautiful, steep mountain. New levels are exciting to talk about. But when we start the climb, the reality of what we are facing begins to appear. Some of the forerunners who have gone before us often tell stories of the difficulties and dangers on the path up to the new level.

We read about the successes of forerunners in the Charismatic Movement but most times don't realize the challenges they faced. On April 3, 1960, when Dennis Bennett, a priest in the Episcopal Church in Van Nuys, California, testified before the congregation that he had received the baptism of the Holy Spirit, he was asked to resign. The prominent 2,600-member congregation, St. Mark's Episcopal, was featured in *Newsweek* and *Time* magazines. Bennett decided to resign his pastorate rather than subject the members to the media frenzy. He continued his ministry at St. Luke's Episcopal Church in Seattle, Washington. He and his wife Rita became prominent in founding the Episcopal Renewal Ministries. Bennett wrote books about his experience that went around the world. He and hundreds of others were empowered to wear their new mantles.

Mantles were worn by prophets in the Old Testament. Paula Price in her book, *The Prophet's Dictionary*, describes a mantle this way.

> A loose-fitting garment worn by prophets and other officials in authority to signify their position and power to exercise dominion. Mantles reflect latitude, stature, prestige, and provisions of the wearer, as well as the license to act.[3]

Today, prophets do not usually wear visible mantles of fabric. They are wearing mantles that are spiritual and not visible to the eyes of people. Yet, mantles of cloth or other materials are bestowed on the person as a symbolic

---

[3] Paula A. Price, *The Prophet's Dictionary* (Tulsa, OK: Flaming Vision Publications, 2002), 328.

gesture of what is happening spiritually. There is a transference of spiritual authority as the mantle is released.

Mantles Released to Younger Generation

The Old Testament is filled with accounts of people who received mantles that prepared them to be successful in their God-given assignments on Earth. One of these people was Moses who released his mantle to Joshua. Joshua had been a warrior under the leadership of Moses. He walked close to Moses. He observed Moses when he spent time in the presence of the Lord. Joshua observed the brightness of the glory of God that caused the face of Moses to shine after he had been with the Lord. Truly, Moses was a prophet chosen by God to lead His people into the promise of the Lord.

The time had come for Moses to transfer his mantle to a spiritual son. God spoke to Moses from His Council Room to name the heir to his mantle.

> The Lord said to Moses, "Behold, the time for you to die is near; call Joshua and present yourselves at the tent of meeting, that I may commission him." So, Moses and Joshua went and presented themselves at the tent of meeting.
>
> Deuteronomy 31:14

> Joshua the son of Nun was filled with the spirit of wisdom, for Moses had laid his hands on him; and the sons of Israel listened to him and did as the Lord had commanded Moses.
>
> Deuteronomy 34:9

Joshua could no longer be merely an observer of a powerful prophet. His time had arrived. He must now be clothed with his own mantle to reach his destiny. Every prophet and prophetic person must be clothed with their individual prophetic mantle. They cannot merely watch other prophets and hope to function in the same way as the prophet. A fresh prophetic mantle is needed to cause the person to shift into their prophetic destiny. Often the release of this mantle is done through prophecy and the laying on of hands. The Old Testament records the time when Elijah transferred his mantle to Elisha.

> Elisha the son of Shaphat of Abel-mecholah you shall anoint as prophet in your place. So, he departed from there and found Elisha the son of Shaphat, while he was plowing with twelve pairs of oxen before him, and he with the twelfth. And Elijah passed over to him and threw his mantle on him.
>
> 1 Kings 19:16, 19

Elijah heard the direction of the Lord from the Council Room. The mantle signified there had been a shift in Elisha's life. He was entering into a new future. It was time for Elisha to follow the prophet, so he could receive the full measure God had for him. The mantle signifies a spiritual deposit in the person's life. However, the person must be willing to yield to God's call. Often, that involves sacrifices. It involves warfare. Faith is tested in the furnace of affliction. Will the prophetic person quit or believe that the mantle of the Lord empowers them to fulfill their prophetic purpose?

I wrote in my book, *Empowered for Your Purpose*,[4] about going through the fiery furnaces and deep waters.

> Not only are we refined and chosen in the furnace of affliction, but we are there for another purpose. The Lord releases a greater level of authority in our lives. We go through the furnace to teach the furnace a lesson—that we can go through the fire and not be burned! We go through the waters to teach the waters a lesson—that we will not be drowned! We encounter the roaring lion to teach the lion a lesson—that there is a lion of the tribe of Judah, and He has prevailed.
>
> Revelation 5:5, *paraphrased*

As we move forward in God's purpose, sometimes it is difficult to break out of the old places. Hidden areas must be dealt with. These areas are enemies that keep us from the Lord's success. When moving forward out of the old place and going into the new level of authority, there are times when it seems we are not making progress. Just before breakthrough, there can be a time of standing still. God causes us to stand still and face the enemies that have followed us. The time of standing still is not designed by the Lord to cause us misery but, rather to set us free. During this time of testing, some describe it as a furnace of affliction. Others describe it as navigating in deep, troubled waters. But God promises us success. We

[4] Barbara Wentroble, *Empowered for Your Purpose* (Dallas, TX: Creative Press, 2014), 177.

are to stand still and trust Him to carry us up to the next level.

The Double Portion

A new level of authority was needed for Elisha to be successful as a prophet. He had asked Elijah to give him a double portion of his spirit.

> It came about when they had crossed over, that Elijah said to Elisha, "Ask what I shall do for you before I am taken from you." And Elisha said, "Please, let a double portion of your spirit be upon me."
>
> 2 Kings 2:9

Asking for the double portion was asking for the inheritance of the firstborn. In Old Testament days, firstborn sons were given twice the inheritance of the other sons (Deuteronomy 21:17). The Bible promises believers today have a prophetic promise of the double portion of the firstborn.

> You will be called the priests of the LORD; You will be spoken of as ministers of our God. You will eat the wealth of nations, and in their riches you will boast. [Or Glory]. Instead of your shame you will have a double portion, and instead of humiliation they will shout for joy over their portion. Therefore they will possess a double portion in their land, Everlasting joy will be theirs.
>
> Isaiah 61:6-7

Contend for Prophetic Promise

Prophets and prophetic people must contend for this promise. I grew up spiritually in an area that did not believe in prophets for today. They also did not believe in women holding any type of spiritual authority or leadership. I spent many years pressing through the religious resistance in that area. Somehow, I knew God had a better future for me than what I was experiencing. I knew the only way to fail was to quit. The promise from the Lord was that He would give the double portion to me if I would believe Him and keep moving forward. Today, that promise has manifested. God has the Isaiah 61:6-7 promise for every prophet and every prophetic believer!

Elisha had to contend for God's promises for his life. He knew that he would be the successor to the ministry of Elijah. He knew he would need a greater portion of spiritual authority and anointing to fulfill his call. Elisha knew he would have great responsibilities and face great dangers and difficulties. He was not asking for a public show to make himself look good before the crowds. Elisha was humble enough to know that he needed a greater portion of supernatural help to follow in the steps of his spiritual father. This was a strategic time, and Elisha was bold enough to make the request.

Later, Elisha stood by the Jordan River as Elijah was taken up to Heaven. Elijah's mantle fell at the feet of Elisha. It was time for him to have his faith tested. There may not have been any emotional indication that a transference of power had taken place. It was merely a knowing that spiritual power had entered him to accomplish God's will on Earth. A prophet or prophetic person does not need to *feel* that they are anointed. They must believe that God has been faithful to fulfill His word in their lives. Others will soon see the evidence of the mantling of the Lord! They will see something has happened that has never happened in the life of that person before!

Elisha also took up the mantle of Elijah that fell from him and returned and stood by the bank of the Jordan.

> He took the mantle of Elijah that fell from him, and struck the waters and said, "Where is the Lord, the God of Elijah?" And when he also had stuck the waters, they were divided here and there; and Elisha crossed over. When the sons of the prophets who were at Jericho opposite him saw him, they said, "The spirit of Elijah rests on Elisha." They came to meet him and bowed themselves to the ground before him.
>
> 2 Kings 2:13-15

New Covenant Mantles

Not only were mantles released in the Old Testament. The New Testament reveals the promise of mantles for New Covenant believers. The Upper Room became the door to God's Council Room at Pentecost. As the 120 followers of Jesus gathered in unity for prayer, Heaven invaded Earth!

> Suddenly there came from heaven a noise like a violent, rushing wind, and it filled the whole house where they were sitting. There appeared to them tongues as of fire

> distributing themselves, and they rested
> on each one of them. They were all filled
> with the Holy Spirit and began to speak
> with other tongues, as the Spirit was
> giving them utterance.
>
> Acts 2:2-4

Like Joshua and Elisha of old, these believers would need supernatural power to fulfill God's purposes on Earth. The door to the Council Room opened as they prayed. They knew they had been told to wait until they were mantled with power through the Holy Spirit. The problem was, they didn't know what that would look like. It is perplexing when we know a change has taken place but don't know what the actual experience will be like. Their responsibility was to stay in God's Council Room, the Upper Room, until they received the mantling of the Holy Spirit. They would know they received a new mantle because of the change in their lives. Others would see the effect of this new mantle. Like those who observed the empowering of Elisha's mantle, people witnessed the manifestation of the newly released mantles at Pentecost.

> They all continued in amazement and
> great perplexity, saying to one another,
> "What does this mean?"
>
> Acts 2:12

Peter, in the past season, had been one who spoke out of turn. I call Peter's raucous behavior Foot in Mouth Disease. Open mouth and insert foot! He said the wrong thing at the right time! However, Pentecost caused a shift in Peter's life. Jesus promised this shift to His followers. Believers would be mantled for extraordinary feats through the power of the Holy Spirit.

> You shall receive power when the Holy
> Spirit has come upon you; and you shall
> be My witnesses both in Jerusalem and in
> all Judea and Samaria, even to the
> remotest part of the earth.
>
> Acts 1:8

Suddenly, Peter was mantled for his prophetic destiny. He boldly spoke to the crowds to explain the mantling of the Lord through the outpouring of the Holy Spirit. This is what was spoken of through the prophet Joel.

> "AND IT SHALL BE IN THE LAST
> DAYS," God says, "THAT I WILL
> POUR FORTH OF MY SPIRIT UPON
> ALL MANKIND; AND YOUR SONS
> AND YOUR DAUGHTERS SHALL
> PROPHESY, AND YOUR YOUNG
> MEN SHALL SEE VISIONS, AND
> YOUR OLD MEN SHALL DREAM
> DREAMS; EVEN UPON MY
> BONDSLAVES, BOTH MEN AND
> WOMEN I WILL IN THOSE DAYS
> POUR FORTH OF MY SPIRIT and they
> shall prophesy."
>
> Acts 2:16-18

A new era had arrived! New Covenant followers would now have access to prophetic mantles from the Lord. They would receive power to accomplish God's will for their lives. Like the Early Church that was mantled with the Holy Spirit, believers today can receive power to shift them from who they have been in the past to who God created them to be.

When I received the Holy Spirit, I was changed from the bashful, timid and fearful person I had always been to the bold person I am today. God's prophetic mantle has the power to change a person from who they think they are to who God intends for them to be!

The early followers of Jesus were spoken of as those who turned the world upside down (Acts 17:6). The world needs a prophetic company of people to turn today's world upside down! As a believer, you can be part of that company. You are part of the church of the firstborn and a legal heir to the double portion prophetic mantle! Allow the King of Glory to mantle you for your prophetic assignment!

Practical Steps

1. Describe a time when you sensed the Lord was releasing something inside you, but you didn't understand what was happening?
2. How did you come to an understanding that the Lord has a prophetic call on your life?
3. Explain how people see you different today than they did in your past.
4. Describe your experience in being filled with the Holy Spirit.
5. How have you contended for the prophetic mantle that the Lord has for your life?

CHAPTER 3

Hindrances to Prophetic Ministry

For many years, Dale and I lived with our children in an area that did not believe in prophets, God's supernatural manifestations or women in ministry. Most people in that area believed that divine healings, prophets and apostles were part of the New Testament Church. However, they believed that none of that functioned in today's church.

After the infilling of the Holy Spirit, I had an intense desire to read the Bible and pray. Each day I would spend hours in prayer and reading my Bible. While reading scriptures, I discovered that the Lord promised His Holy Spirit was for all generations. I also discovered that when Jesus ascended to Heaven, after His death, burial and resurrection, He gave gifts to His people. These people were called apostles, prophets, evangelists, pastors and teachers (Ephesians 4:11). He did not say that these gifts were only for the Early Church. Yet, many Christians today believe that several of these gifts no longer function. They believe that apostles and prophets ceased to exist after the completion of the New Testament. I couldn't understand how people are able to believe in three of the gifts: evangelists, pastors and teachers but not believe in two of the gifts, apostles and prophets. From a common-sense point of view, it didn't make sense. If pastors, evangelists and teachers still function today, why are prophets and apostles no longer functioning?

Hindrance from Mindsets

Knowing the mindset that was prevalent in our area produced challenges for me. The challenges included a choice I needed to make. Would I be obedient to the Lord or remain silent? Prophets and prophetic people usually face similar challenges. To obey the Lord even when facing challenges requires determination.

Our church pressed through the doctrine of unbelief in prophetic ministry while living in that area. Many people had become accustomed to prophecy. Sunday mornings were powerful as prophecy was released to strengthen and build up our church. During that time, we had a new pastor come to the church. He was from a church that was very active in the prophetic. He seemed like a good fit for our congregation.

Hindrance from Intimidation

The pastor had not been with us long before he started making comments each week. He would say, "Someday, the Lord is going to restore the TRUE prophetic." The emphasis was always on the word TRUE. Intimidation seemed to saturate the atmosphere. Many people thought that maybe what they were experiencing was not the real prophetic. People who had been operating prophetically stopped prophesying. It was only a matter of time until I was the only person prophesying.

Before going to church each Sunday, a prophetic word would seem to bubble up inside me. I remember begging the Lord not to ask me to prophesy. I didn't want to be the only person releasing a prophetic word. However, the Lord continued giving me a prophetic word each Sunday. I wanted to be obedient to the Lord. But I continued to battle with what people might be thinking. I reached the point of dreading to go to church. I kept thinking that I didn't want people to feel "Here comes Barbara. She has another prophecy this week." They didn't say that, but I was afraid they might be sensing that thought. Throughout that time, the pastor continued making the statement, "Someday, the Lord is going to restore the TRUE prophetic." He did not forbid people to prophesy. However, his words were enough to intimidate people so they quit using their prophetic gifts.

What a battle I was in! During one of those times as I stood in the Council Room of the Lord, I continued asking the Lord not to use me in prophecy. He replied to my begging. "Barbara, you are going to prophesy until you don't care what people think." Wow! I realized that I was battling for my future. Being obedient to the Lord needed to be my concern rather than the opinions of people. God was challenging me to be free from intimidation and fear. I decided that I would do what the Lord was asking me to do. If He wanted me to prophesy each week, I would obey. From that point on, I no longer focused on what people were thinking. I merely listened for the prophetic word from the Lord that would be a blessing to the hearers.

It didn't take long after that for the Lord to release me from prophesying each week. It seemed that I had passed the test I was in! I then understood the reason for the battle. There was a place in me that the Lord needed to free me from. He knew the future. If I continued carrying the baggage of intimidation and fear, I would not be able to be obedient to the Lord. He could not fully accomplish what He wanted to do with me in the future. There are times when we must contend against hindrances designed to stop the gift the Lord has put inside His people.

Hindrance from Religious Spirits

Another hindrance that prophets and prophetic people often encounter is a religious spirit. Peter Wagner defined this spirit in his book, *Freedom from the Religious Spirit.* "The spirit of religion is an agent of Satan assigned to prevent change and maintain the status quo by using religious devices."[5]

This spirit can be compared to the Pharisees, a religious sect that was active during the time of Jesus. They are usually described as a group of religious leaders who were insistent on fulfilling the literal details of the Mosaic Law. They were insensitive to the spiritual significance of the Law. The Pharisees operated in legalism rather than a personal relationship with God. Pharisees were always a hindrance to Jesus and His ministry. Jesus had strong words to the Pharisees.

> Woe to you, scribes and Pharisees, hypocrites! For you are like whitewashed tombs which on the outside appear beautiful, but inside they are full of dead men's bones and all uncleanness. Even so you too outwardly appear righteous to men, but inwardly you are full of hypocrisy and lawlessness.

---

[5] C. Peter Wagner, General Editor, *Freedom from the Religious Spirit* (Ventura, CA: Regal Books, 2005), 12.

Matthew 23:27-28

A religious spirit will seek to hinder a person from the free expression of the Spirit of God. It keeps a prophet from sensing not merely the words of prophecy but also the heart of the Lord. A prophet or prophetic person must be able to deliver the word of the Lord through the heart of the Lord. Judgmental and angry words delivered to people obediently serving the Lord are not from the heart of God. Those words come from a religious spirit.

I remember a time when the Lord helped me realize that I had a religious spirit. Dale and I were vacationing in Florida with another ministry couple. We decided to visit Bishop Bill Hamon's church on a Friday night. The atmosphere was charged with excitement. People were dancing and singing during the time of worship. The worship leader encouraged us to sing a new song he had recently written.

Council Room Freedom

As the people were singing the song, I realized that I was struggling with the words. I couldn't get the words to the song out of my mouth. The name of the song was *Rocking in the Holy of Holies*! Suddenly, I found myself in the Council Room of the Lord. (See my book, *Accessing the Power of God.*) He revealed the source of my dilemma. The religious spirit in me refused to participate in a song that was different from my religious background. I was legalistic in trying to prove the song was scriptural rather than understanding the heart of joy and worship from the song. The Lord is faithful to reveal hindrances that can contaminate our prophetic ministry.

I remember turning to my ministry friend and whispering in his ear, "I can't sing that song. I think that I have a religious spirit!" I loved the Lord. I loved being used in prophetic ministry. Yet, I could not enjoy a song that my legalistic mind was hindering. I wanted a chapter and verse from the Bible that said it was okay to rock in the Holy of Holies! I couldn't remember any verse in the Bible that said I could do this.

After the meeting, I quickly went to the church bookstore. I asked the attendant to tell me which CD had that song on it. I bought it to take home with me. I was determined to listen to the song over and over. The Lord had revealed that I had a religious spirit. I would now do whatever it took to be delivered from a religious spirit. Sometimes, we must take radical steps to free ourselves from any religious spirit that is seeking to hinder our prophetic gift.

To be victorious, we must allow the Lord to change some of the old mindsets. The Christian walk is not free from the fiery darts of the enemy. We must not be like some who think that the enemy only attacks those who are walking in disobedience to the Lord. Our battles are against the evil strongholds on Earth. In the midst of our battles, we have the confidence from the Lord that we are on the winning side. The Lord has promised,

> The kingdom of the world has become
> the kingdom of our Lord and His Christ;
> and He will reign forever and ever.
> Revelation 11:15

Hindrance from the Jezebel Spirit

Another hindrance to prophetic ministry is the Jezebel spirit. Jesus warned the church at Thyatira about this evil spirit.

> I have this against you, that you tolerate
> the woman Jezebel, who calls herself a
> prophetess, and she teaches and leads My
> bondservants astray, so that they commit
> acts of immorality and eat things
> sacrificed to idols.
>
> Revelation 2:20

Jezebel is a picture of a woman in scripture (1 Kings 19). When the spirit is in operation, it is neither male nor female. It can operate in men or women. We usually use the pronoun "she" due to the picture of Jezebel as a woman in scripture. Jezebel usually targets leadership or people in strategic places. She comes with flattering words and is usually highly gifted. Jezebel knows how to use the scriptures to seem like a very spiritual person. She may even prophesy accurate words over you. Her prophetic gift may appear stronger than your gift.

As the relationship between you and Jezebel develops, this spirit changes. Now, she turns into a controlling and angry person. She will make you feel guilty if you do not obey her commands. Sometimes, she will say to you, "After all I have done for you. Now, look at how you are treating me." When guilt doesn't work, she releases her anger. The anger is so fierce a person will usually be hesitant to say anything to try to bring peace. You then must deal with feelings of rejection. Recognize witchcraft is working to entangle you in her web of control. That spirit is attempting to steal even your ability to make your own decisions. Jezebel wants you dependent on her. Because of Jezebel's influence in your life, you are filled with fear, rejection and confusion. You feel like you are in a stupor or having a bad dream. What happened to this person that I thought I had a good relationship with? Your mind and emotions are in turmoil. The relationship was deceptive and involved a demon spirit rather than merely a person. When you recognize a Jezebel spirit operating in your life–run! Get away from that spirit. Find someone that can pray with you to break any of Jezebel's power off your life. God has a better future for you than what you are experiencing with Jezebel!

Jezebel hated God's prophets. She had her own prophets, but they were false. She threatened the prophet Elijah with death. Even though Elijah was a powerful prophet, Jezebel invoked fear into his life. Elijah ran from the woman. After his journey away from Jezebel, he lay down under a juniper tree. At that place, Elijah experienced the Council Room of the Lord. The Council Room can be anyplace the Lord chooses. It is not limited to a church building or some religious structure. God loves to establish His Council Room in the most unexpected places–even under a juniper tree!

Elijah was touched by an angel of the Lord and given nourishment and instructions for his assignment. Later, Elijah had another Council Room meeting with the Lord at Horeb (1 Kings 19). The Lord gave instructions that included anointing Jehu as king over Israel. Jehu later killed Jezebel in fulfillment of the prophetic word given to Elijah. Jehu also killed the false prophets and their followers. Jezebel has power but not as much power as the Lord and His anointed prophets!

Difference in False Prophets and False Prophecy

The Jezebel spirit is a picture of the woman Jezebel in the scriptures. That spirit can operate in anyone willing to be used by the enemy. A Jezebel spirit operates in false prophets. There is a difference between false prophets and a false prophecy. A false prophet operates under the power of Satan. The person tries to appear as a real prophet when they are not. They prophesy when the Lord has not spoken.

> The Lord of hosts says, "Do not listen to the words of the prophets who are prophesying to you. They are leading you into futility; they speak a vision of their own imagination, not from the mouth of the Lord."
>
> Jeremiah 23:16

A true prophet can give a false prophecy. The person simply misses what the Lord is saying. The prophet loves the Lord, studies the scriptures and has a heart for God. The prophet simply is an imperfect person. God uses that person anyway. I believe the Lord sometimes allows true prophets to miss what He is saying. He wants them to always lean on Him and listen more deeply to His voice. This is a learning experience! Failing to deliver the right prophetic word shows that only Jesus is perfect. He never missed it! God has chosen to use imperfect people for His purposes. How wonderful that today's prophets are not stoned for missing the right word!

The false prophets use enticing words to draw people to themselves. The power of their carnal words is used to gain control over unsuspecting people. Sometimes these false prophets charge large fees for their prophecies. They even use scripture to justify the financial fees.

Hindrances from False Prophets
Years ago, I was ministering in a city with my friend,

Chuck Pierce. When he stood to speak, he said there was a window over the city. He said the window would open and then it would close. He then said he did not know why the window would close but that is what he saw. I had only ministered a few times in that city. Therefore, I did not know what was happening in the churches or the meetings in that area.

While Chuck was speaking, I stepped into the Council Room of the Lord. The Council Room is a spiritual place and not a physical place. John experienced this place on the Isle of Patmos. He described his experience in the Book of Revelation. "I was in the Spirit on the Lord's day, and I heard behind me a loud voice like *the sound* of a trumpet" (Revelation 1:10). Prophets and prophetic people experience conversations with the Lord in His Council Room.

Later in the meeting, Chuck asked me to come to the front and help him minister to the people. When I came, I told the people I felt the Lord had given me revelation concerning the opening and closing of the window over the city. I referred to the scripture that talks about false prophets coming to the homes of widows, taking their money and saying, "Thus says the Lord" when the Lord did not speak.

> They shamelessly cheat widows out of their property and then pretend to be pious by making long prayers in public. Because of this, they will be severely punished.
>
> Luke 20:47 NLT

I said false prophets had come to the churches in their city. They had taken money from the people. If they would call these people "false prophets" and not justify them, God would forgive them and open the prophetic window over their city. The window kept closing because of the false prophetic operating in the city. God was trying to open a prophetic window. The Body of Christ needed to stop the prophetic defilement that was occurring in the churches.

When I spoke that, the host of the conference came to the front crying. She said that what I said was true. Prophets had come to the city. They had "$1,000 lines" for people to get into if they wanted a really good prophecy. They had "$100 lines" for people who wanted just a good prophecy. She went on to say when the people did not step in either of the lines, the false prophet intimidated them. The speaker would ask the audience, "Where is your faith?"

The host continued the story of what happened in the city the week before. A false prophet came asking for large sums of money to receive a great prophecy. A widow had just received money from her recently deceased husband. She gave the false prophet the $50,000 that she had just received from his inheritance. The finances in the meetings were so large that a disagreement broke out between the false prophet and the pastor. The pastor had agreed to split the income from the meetings, 50-50. Since the income was so large, the pastor said he could not allow the prophet to have that much money. Such manipulation was not only in the prophet but also in the pastor!

Repentance for Allowing False Prophets

The host stood with Chuck and I and asked a local pastor to come and repent for allowing this to occur in the churches of the city. After the prayer for repentance and forgiveness, Chuck and I had all the people in the conference line up and let us prophesy over each one. We told them we were not charging anything for the prophecies. They were free! We were breaking the power of the false prophets off the city, so the Lord could open a prophetic window over their city. We prophesied until after midnight. Since that time, the prophetic has been released in that city. False prophets are not more powerful than God's prophets and His prophetic people!

There are many other hindrances to prophetic ministry. These are the only ones I will mention in this book. It is important to realize that there are hindrances designed to stop you from fulfilling your call to prophetic ministry. However, the power of God in you is great enough to overcome any hindrance in your life. Knowing that, you can now move past these hindrances and have your prophetic gift activated. We will talk about you and your prophetic gift in the next chapter.

Practical Steps

1. What have you done to press past the mindsets of people who do not believe in prophetic ministry?
2. What convinced you that prophetic ministry is for today?
3. How do you confront intimidation concerning you and your prophetic call?
4. Have you ever had a relationship that seemed like Jezebel? What did you do?
5. What do you do when you recognize a false prophet is operating?

CHAPTER 4

Activating Your Prophetic Gift

The atmosphere during the time of worship was filled with the presence of the Lord! Suddenly, a lady was standing in front of me. "They won't let me prophesy in this church," she commented. She continued telling me, "Each time I want to prophesy, they tell me to give the word to one of the leaders. When the leader gives the word, it is not the same as me giving the word." I could sense she was irritated and pressing me to give her permission to deliver a prophetic word.

I encouraged her to make an appointment with one of the church leaders. She needed to find out what the protocol is in the church for delivering a prophetic word. She continued her dialogue by saying that she was able to prophesy in all the churches she had been in before. My response was that she was not in all the churches she had been in before. The conversation continued for a while. When I would not give her permission to prophesy, she finally left and went to her seat. I don't ever remember seeing her at church again. When she found that she could not just show up and be given permission to prophesy to the congregation, she probably went looking for a church that would allow her to do that.

How sad that many gifted people have not been properly trained and activated for prophetic ministry. The lady may have had a great prophetic call on her life. However, an independent and self-promoting spirit can be dangerous in the Body of Christ. People sometimes feel they must obey what they think is the voice of the Lord without any restrictions. They often feel they deserve special privileges and are exempt from any requirements from leadership.

School of Prophets

A prophetic gift is valuable in the Body of Christ. One of the reasons I developed and taught Schools of the Prophets for many years is to help young prophets and prophetic people to become activated in their gifting. I want them to understand the proper protocol for delivering a prophetic word. I also want them to develop the character needed to fulfill the potential God has for them in their calling. I want to see them succeed! I don't want them to experience unnecessary casualties along the way. God has a better way than to merely learn by trial and error!

Schools of the Prophets can be found as far back as the Old Testament. The prophet Samuel was the first person listed in the Bible to establish a School of Prophets. Prior to Samuel, we find prophetic utterance released through individual prophets. Samuel was probably the first prophet to multiply himself through apprenticeship and training of young prophets. These trained ones became known as "sons of the prophets."

Ernest B. Gentile gives a *good* description of the "sons of prophets" in his book, *Your Sons and Daughters*

Shall Prophesy.[6]

> These "sons" were pupils or disciples of (not literal children of) a prophet. The instructor or leader was considered a spiritual or prophetic "father" (2 Kings 2:12). The sons of the prophets were those disciples of the prophets who devoted themselves studiously to this ministry, sometimes acting as the messengers or ministers to carry out the direction of their leaders.

Spiritual Fathers and Mentors

The Lord never intended for His people to fulfill their earthly assignments alone. He planned for natural parents. Adam and Eve were the first physical parents that God put on Earth. Their first assignment was to be fruitful and multiply (Genesis 1:28). Being fruitful and multiplying would first be through their children. Throughout the Bible, parents were given the task of training their children for possessing their inheritance from the Lord.

> You shall teach them to your sons, talking of them when you sit in your house and when you walk along the road and when you lie down and when you rise up.
> Deuteronomy 11:19

In a similar way, God provides mentors and teachers to help prophetic people mature both in their gifting and in

---

[6] Ernest B. Gentile, *Your Sons and Daughters Shall Prophesy* (Grand Rapids, MI, 1999), 65.

their character. There is a difference between spiritual parents and spiritual mentors. Sometimes they can be the same person. Yet, often they are different people fulfilling different roles. The Apostle Paul addressed the church at Corinth. He reminded them that he was more than a mentor to them. He helped them understand his role, not only as an apostle, but also as the spiritual father of that church.

> If you were to have countless tutors in Christ, yet you would not *have* many fathers; for in Christ Jesus I became your father through the gospel.
>
> 1 Corinthians 4:15

When I use the term "father," I am not necessarily referring to the male gender. In the same way, when I refer to "sons," I am not necessarily referring to young men. For simplicity, I am using the term "father" to refer to a spiritual parent. I use the term "son" to refer to a spiritually young person. Each of these people can be either male or female.

We are living in what many times is described as a "fatherless generation." Too many men and women do not have a natural father. Often, when they do have a natural father, the relationship is distant or non-existent. God created a place in the heart of every person to be filled with a father's love and acceptance. Jesus often referred to God as "Father." He experienced the love and validation of the father before He began His earthly ministry. The heavens parted and the door to the Council Room of the Lord opened. Jesus heard His father speak from the Council Room.

Behold, a voice out of the heavens, saying, "This is My beloved Son, in whom I am well-pleased."

Matthew 3:17

Fathers Involve Relationship

Like Jesus, prophetic people today need validation and acceptance from a father. Spiritual fathers and mothers can fill that need. A spiritual parent should prophesy destiny into a son or daughter. These spiritual parents have access to the Council Room of the Lord. They can hear the destiny that God has for these spiritual children. The prophetic word of destiny will destroy the sense of illegitimacy or abandonment. Jacob prophesied the future destiny of each of his twelve sons.

Jacob summoned his sons and said, "Assemble yourselves that I may tell you what shall befall you in the days to come."

Genesis 49:1

A spiritual father is joined to the young prophet out of a heart relationship. I once heard a leader say, "Don't ever let someone cover (father) you unless that person loves you." Spiritual parents are not people who merely put your name on a list of members or on a document. These are people who know you in the pulpit and out of the pulpit. They are with you in the good times and through the storms of life.

Spiritual fathers love you enough to encourage the activation of your prophetic gift. They want the best for your life. They see the potential in you that you may not see in yourself. Ask the Lord to place a spiritual parent in your life. Cling to that parent. Realize they love you enough to stretch you, correct you and believe you have a prophetic destiny to be fulfilled!

Mentors Are Teachers

There are times when a prophetic person may need a mentor. A spiritual mentor is often a teacher. A good mentor wants the disciple to go farther in life than he has gone. He wants that prophetic person to walk in greater authority and power than he has experienced. There should be no jealousy. There is only joy and celebration as that spiritual son ascends to a higher level of prophetic activation.

You may have many prophetic mentors in life. Some of these mentors, you will meet face to face. Others may come through books, conference speakers, media, and other sources. Your gift can be activated as you respond to the teaching or equipping. There may or may not be a relationship involved. Be sure to understand the difference between your spiritual father and your mentor. Fathers are for a lifetime. Mentors may be temporary and occasional. They may be in your life for a period to equip you to fulfill a specific assignment. However, prophetic mentors are valuable in activating people for prophetic ministry. They help to establish biblical foundations. They help unlock the prophetic treasures God has placed in you!

Prophets and Prophetic People

The New Testament tells us all believers can be used to prophesy. "For you can all prophesy one by one; so that all may learn and all may be exhorted" (1 Corinthians 14:31). Prophecy is a life-giving force that breaks people out of hopelessness and despair. It gives them hope for the future. Prophecy is also used to reveal the thoughts and heart of God to His people. Every believer can enjoy the privilege of releasing this river of life to God's people.

Not every believer is a prophet. There are times when a prophetic person may desire to prophesy in the way he sees a prophet operate. The young prophetic person may sense a word of correction, ministry confirmation or revelation. These aspects of prophecy should come from a recognized prophet. Seasoned prophets have the maturity and experience to release those words with the proper protocol and in the Lord's timing.

Ways to Know You Are A Prophet

Dale and I were members of a church years ago that wanted to train young prophets and prophetic people. I was asked to help with the prophetic training. This church established three ways for a person to know if they were a recognized prophet in that church.

First, the person would know inside themselves that God had the call of a prophet on their life. They would sense God wanted them to do more than operate in the gift of prophecy. They would have words of knowledge, words of wisdom and discerning of spirits operating in their life. These revelation gifts operate frequently and accurately in prophets.

The second way the person would know that they were called to be a prophet is others would recognize the call. People would say they believed the person was called to be a prophet. People would ask to receive prophetic ministry from that person.

The third way the person would know that they were a prophet is that the church would publicly recognize the person as a prophet. Sometimes there would be a commissioning of the person. Other times, the person would merely be mentioned from the pulpit as a prophet. Understanding the recognition of how prophets are affirmed helped prevent misunderstanding of the different roles of prophets and prophetic people. Not every church uses this system. However, a way of identifying prophets can prevent unnecessary confusion.

The prophet stands in the Council Room of the Lord and hears the prophetic word from the Father. Prophets also activate prophetic gifts in God's people. The Apostle Paul reminded his spiritual son, Timothy, to activate the spiritual gifts imparted to him.

> For this reason I remind you to kindle afresh the gift of God which is in you through the laying on of hands.
>
> 2 Timothy 1:6

Timothy's spiritual father had laid hands on Timothy. He activated the gift in Timothy, so he could be successful in his God-given assignment. Your spiritual father or a prophet can activate the prophetic gift God put in you.

Spirit of Prophecy

Another way to have the prophetic gift in you activated is through a gathering of prophetic people. I encourage people to "stay around the anointing." That means to stay around prophets and prophetic people. Often, the Spirit of Prophecy will be released in corporate prophetic settings. "The testimony of Jesus is the spirit of prophecy" (Revelation 19:10). When the Spirit of Prophecy is active in a group of people, anyone can prophesy. People who do not normally prophesy can prophesy by using a small amount of faith. Prophetic gifts are activated during these times. Believers can strengthen, encourage and comfort one another.

Believers can enter God's Council Room. They can hear God's thoughts toward His children. God's thoughts are really what prophecy is! Believers can release those thoughts that God has toward His children. He is a good father who thinks good things about His sons and daughters! As a believer, you are destined to release the thoughts of Father God into the Earth!

Destined for Kingdom Purposes

Father God has a prophetic destiny for you. You may not know what the destiny is. At this time, you may not understand God's purpose for your life. You are not a victim of circumstances. You may not have had perfect opportunities in life to prepare you for your destiny. However, God has a generation of people on Earth who march to the beat of a different drummer. They do not allow circumstances and difficulties to stop them from pursuing their God-given destiny.

These prophetic people are willing to step out in faith. They connect with spiritual mothers and fathers. They prepare for their future by listening to mentors. They attend Schools of Prophets to build a solid foundation for their prophetic call.

Voice of the Lord from the Council Room

You are part of this powerful prophetic generation arising on Earth! Spend time in the Council Room of the Lord. Learn to fine tune your spirit to the voice of the Lord. His voice is the key to your destiny.

Several years ago, my husband and I were travelling with another ministry couple. We would be leading a prayer conference in another state. On our way to the conference, we decided to step into the Council

Room of the Lord. (We didn't know that was what it was called at that time!). We would listen to see what the Lord was speaking to each of us.

I carefully got my pen and writing tablet. We didn't have iPads at that time. As I stepped into God's Council Room, I heard Him so loud in my spirit. He said something that has propelled me into my destiny. "Barbara, teach My people to hear My voice." The voice was not audible for others to hear. Yet, it was so loud that I could not miss the voice of the Lord.

From that point on, I knew what my mission in life was. Whatever I would be doing in the future would always include this purpose–teaching people to hear the voice of the Lord! In fact, my mission statement today includes this–to educate, equip and empower. I fulfill this mission by helping raise up a prophetic generation of people in churches, the marketplace, businesses, government, and all the seven mountains of culture.

You have your prophetic gift activated by walking in the areas covered in this chapter. You are qualified to step into the Council Room of the Lord. Allow your activated prophetic gift to hear the voice of the Lord concerning your destiny. God has a future and a hope for you!

> "There is hope for your future," declares the Lord.
>
> Jeremiah 31:17

Your future and destiny as a prophetic person may be in the marketplace. We will discuss this calling in the next chapter!

Practical Steps

1. Articulate the protocol for delivering a prophetic word in your church, Bible study or other Christian gathering that you attend.
2. What is the value of a School of Prophets?
3. How can a spiritual parent break the power of a "fatherless spirit"?
4. Describe the difference between a mentor and a spiritual parent.
5. List a few ways that a person can know if they are a prophet.

CHAPTER 5

Prophetic in the Marketplace

I was excited about the upcoming conference I was sponsoring! The conference would focus on God using His people in the marketplace. At that time, I was not aware of anyone holding conferences on that topic. We have always helped pioneer fresh new moves of God's Spirit. This would be no different!

My friend, Peter Wagner, was one of the speakers. He was excited to be included. Peter loved exploring the new! "Barbara, I am a little nervous about speaking at this conference," Peter remarked. "I have never spoken at a marketplace conference before." I couldn't imagine Peter being nervous about anything! He was such a brave, adventurous person! Later, Peter became known around the world for encouraging marketplace people.

We knew we were helping to launch a fresh move of God. Others were probably doing similar things in other places. We were just not aware of it. On the first day of the conference, I was handed a secular magazine for business people. The cover article was titled, *Faith in the Workplace*. The article included stories from several people who wrote how their faith helped them at work.

These people were from various religious faiths. Wow! Even the secular world was getting the message!

Since that time, I have continued to teach and encourage people in the workplace. One of my desires is to help them develop a biblical worldview. That worldview includes an understanding that God does not live exclusively in a church building. He is throughout Earth and communicates with mankind wherever they are. "The heavens are telling of the glory of God; and their expanse is declaring the work of His hands" (Psalm 19:1).

First Person in Bible Filled with Spirit

The Bible is filled with accounts of God using people in the marketplace. The first person the Bible described as filled with the Spirit or being anointed was a marketplace worker. Moses stood in the Council Room of the Lord to receive instructions on building the Tabernacle of Moses. He could not merely come up with a good idea. He could not even choose close friends or family members to hire for the building project. He needed the word of the Lord for constructing a place to house the Lord's presence.

As Moses stood in the Lord's Council Room, God called for a marketplace person to build this glorious structure.

> The Lord spoke to Moses, saying, "See, I have called by name Bezalel, the son of Uri, the son of Hur, of the tribe of Judah. And I have filled him with the Spirit of God in wisdom, in understanding, in knowledge, and in all kinds of *craftsmanship.*"
>
> Exodus 31:1-3

Bezalel is the first person in the Bible that God called "filled with the Spirit." That means a marketplace person was the first person considered "anointed" in the Bible. Bezalel and his co-workers had an ability from the Lord to be successful in their God-given tasks. Bezalel was the chief artisan of the Tabernacle and in charge of building the Ark of the Covenant.

The principle of "first mention" in the Bible is significant. When something in the Bible is mentioned for the first time, we need to pay attention to it. That means God wants us to pay attention to people in the marketplace and His Spirit's empowering for their lives.

Zebulun Tribe

We also notice that there were twelve tribes of Israel. The tribe of Zebulun is the only tribe mentioned as having an "undivided heart."

> Of Zebulun, there were 50,000 who went out in the army, who could draw up in battle formation with all kinds of weapons of war and helped *David* with an undivided heart.
>
> 1 Chronicles 12:33

Business people can walk with God with an undivided heart. They love God. They also love their work. They do not need to choose between their affection toward God and work. They can love both at the same time. That is what an undivided heart is about!

The Jewish calendar also has meanings for each month. My friend, Chuck Pierce, describes the month of Sivan this way.[7]

> Sivan is associated with the tribe of Zebulun, who was noted for ability in business and the marketplace. Sivan is the "business people's month." God wants you to do some business with Him in the month of Sivan. He wants you to learn prosperity principles.

How amazing that the Lord would describe a business tribe as one with an undivided heart! How awesome that he would mention one tribe as a business tribe. Too often, business people have been labeled as unspiritual. They are made to feel like second-class members in the Body of Christ. God created a tribe and a month that He would use to emphasize the value of business people!

The season of Sivan is the ninth month of the civil year and the third month of the ecclesiastical year on the Hebrew calendar. It is a spring month of 30 days. Sivan usually falls in May–June on the Gregorian calendar.

Business People Receive Their Call in the Council Room

Often, I hear business people tell of the time when they sensed the Lord was calling them to start a business or work in one of the seven mountains of culture. I believe that these people stood in the Council Room of the Lord. They heard Him call them to walk with Him and serve Him with their lives. He called that person to occupy a place in at least one of the seven mountains of culture.

---

[7] Chuck D. Pierce with Robert and Linda Heidler, *A Time to Advance* (Denton, TX: Glory of Zion International, Inc., 2011), 272.

My friend, Lance Wallnau, has made the terminology of seven mountains understandable. He labels these spheres of influence as:

1. Family
2. Religion
3. Government
4. Media
5. Education
6. Business
7. Arts

These same workplace people sometimes struggle later in life with negative feelings. They feel their job is not as significant as a pastor or some other spiritual person. They sometimes feel they have missed the call of God on their lives. They remember standing in the Council Room of the Lord. They sensed His hand on their lives. If God has a call on their lives, that must mean He wants them to pastor a church, travel as a prophet or evangelist or some other spiritual position.

Many times, these individuals leave the workplace in search of what they term *ministry*. In their search for ministry, they often experience failure, defeat and poverty. They were successful in the workplace. Ministry efforts have not been successful. What happened to the call of God on their lives? Is this the life that the Lord called them to? Confusion and discouragement are worn like garments on their lives.

These people were taught that holiness is found inside church buildings. Outside those buildings, in the workplace, the places are unholy. Therefore, their work, their money and their desires to be successful and increase in finances is unholy. Is there a way to live without the desire to create wealth and find success in life? The mind frequently questions these seemingly carnal desires. The person is always looking for deliverance from such unholy thoughts. Like the Apostle Paul, these people wrestle with these negative thoughts.

> For that which I am doing, I do not understand; for I am not practicing what I would like to do, but I am doing the very thing I hate... Wretched man that I am! Who will set me free from the body of this death?
>
> Romans 7:15, 24

Greek Thinking

This type thinking separated spiritual leaders from secular people is founded in what we term as Greek thinking. Our mindsets in the Western world have been shaped by the teachings of Greek philosophers like Plato. He taught a view of the world known as dualism. According to his teaching, the world is divided into two levels. The upper level is called "form." This level includes eternal ideas. This area is superior and the level each person should strive to achieve. The belief is that most of this happens after a person leaves this old, evil world. The goal is to try to survive on evil Earth and wait to get out and live in eternal bliss. This is a place regarded in various religions as the abode of God (or the gods) and the angels, and of the good after death. Often this place is traditionally depicted as being above the sky. Some believe it is a transcendent state known as paradise or nirvana. Christians know Heaven is the location of the throne of God as well as the home of holy angels. Heaven is a physical place in the afterlife.

The lower level consists of "matter." That means anything on Earth, including your work, money, education, economics, politics, etc., are labeled as carnal. Christians are encouraged to stay out of these areas. No ministry is possible in such evil and carnal spheres.

Hebrew Thinking

Hebrew beliefs are different from Greek thinking. Hebrews saw the Lord and His throne, His Council Room, available today. They saw the King of Glory existing over Earth and all creation. Hebrews saw the spiritual and natural, including work, as under the oversight of the Lord. There is no division between the natural realm and spiritual realm. Therefore, workplace people have access to the Council Room of the Lord. This is not a place reserved only for those who function inside church walls! Nor do you need to wait until you get to Heaven to enjoy the privilege of dialoguing, conversing and strategizing with the Lord!

Old Testament Marketplace People

The Bible is filled with testimonies of marketplace people. When we read these true stories without a religious lens, we can see how powerfully God used marketplace people throughout His Word. One marketplace person that God used in the Old Testament was Jacob. Jacob was in the business mountain. He spent most of his life wandering and away from his homeland. Jacob was a crafty schemer. We will not go into the various aspects of his life but look at the blessings of the Lord.

Although Jacob was no saint in his early years, God was faithful. God gave Jacob supernatural wisdom. I believe that is the result of the grace of God. When we are unfaithful, God often is faithful to us. He uses His love and blessings to draw us back to Him. Marketplace people can draw on the grace of God. You may have made mistakes in the past. You may have failed. You may not have served the Lord. I love what Robert Heidler is known for saying. "You can repent!" God is faithful to give people a second chance. He makes a way to start over again. His plan and purpose for your life never changes.

God gave supernatural wisdom to Jacob to break him out of lack and into wealth. I believe Jacob stood in the Council Room of the Lord for this wisdom. He may not have understood what was happening. He may not have heard an audible voice. Yet, he suddenly knew a strategy to break him into wealth for his future (Genesis 30:35-42.) He knew how to take the least, weakest and feeblest animals and turn them into flocks that were valuable.

God sometimes does the same with marketplace people. Suddenly, they have an answer. They know a strategy that can bring God's promise of wealth for their future. They can take whatever is in their hands and turn it into something valuable for increase. Jacob became wealthy despite his circumstances.

> The man became exceedingly prosperous and had large flocks and female and male servants and camels and donkeys.
>
> Genesis 30:43

One more person in the Old Testament is King David. As a king, he was in the government mountain. He had a great prophecy over his life as a young man. He was anointed with oil by the prophet Samuel (1 Samuel 16:13). But David spent years being persecuted, abandoned and even being immoral and becoming a murderer. How could God ever use a person with that profile?

Once again, the grace of God is available to all who call on the Lord. Your defeats, failures and sins are not too hard for God. The blood of Jesus is as powerful for our cleansing and redemption as it was over 2,000 years ago!

David experienced a time of great victory in battle. He woke up one morning after the victory feeling great. His joy must have been tangible. By the end of the day, David hit bottom. When returning home to Ziklag, he discovered that his wives and children had all been captured. The wives and children of his fighting men had also been captured. They were valuable as the town was full of beautiful women, and their children were strong and healthy.

The warriors that had supported and strengthened David turned against him. He was abandoned and left alone. There are times when marketplace people go through great losses. They can sometimes lose everything in a single day. Friends and co-workers desert them. Sometimes even family members can desert them. Times like this seem like the end of the world. The situation may seem hopeless. But God!

David lost everything in a day. It must have felt like a rug was pulled out from under him. Everything was gone. But God! The Bible tells us after David and his warrior men wept out loud, David strengthened himself in the Lord (1 Samuel 30:6). David did this by entering the Council Room of the Lord. That was the only place where David could find supernatural strength to rise up and go again. He received strategy to give him a better tomorrow than what he was experiencing at that time.

David inquired of the Lord in His Council Room.

He asked what he needed to do. God answered David with fresh strategy.

> David inquired of the Lord, saying, "Shall I pursue this band? Shall I overtake them?" And He said to him, "Pursue, for you shall surely over take them, and you shall surely rescue all."
>
> 1 Samuel 30:8

David followed the strategy of the Lord. God's Council Room dialogue promised David that what was lost would be recovered. God has a way of restoring losses for His marketplace people. He promises a future and hope for His children. Nothing is too hard for Him!

David continued in the Lord's strategy. He did not sit down, and only hope God would do what He promised. He was active in pursuing the instructions of the Lord. He knew that if he obeyed his part of the plan that God would fulfill His part. Because of David's obedience, God brought full restoration to David.

> David recovered all that the Amalekites had taken and rescued his two wives. But nothing of theirs was missing, whether small or great, sons or daughters, spoil or anything that they had taken for themselves; David brought it all back.
>
> 1 Samuel 30:18-19

Marketplace People Today

The Lord calls marketplace people today to His Council Room. The Council Room does not need to be inside a church building. This Room is available wherever people work. Just like Jacob and David in the Old Testament, God speaks prophetic words to His marketplace people in the midst of the workplace.

My husband, Dale, has a background as an engineer. He has spent most of his adult life working in various manufacturing plants. Dale is sensitive to the Spirit of the Lord. He also has a strong gift in Word of Knowledge. Word of Knowledge is a prophetic gift. A person has supernatural knowledge about something that they do not know in the natural.

Many times at work in manufacturing plants, a piece of equipment would stop functioning. When the equipment was not working, the hourly workers were sent home without pay. The company also could not meet the deadlines for shipping the products that the company promised for a certain time. Hours without properly working equipment was costly for the employees and the company!

From time to time, the company would call the "experts" in to service the equipment. Frequently, these experts could not find the solution for the equipment. Dale would enter the Council Room of the Lord right in the manufacturing plant. "Lord, what is the cause of this problem with the equipment? What needs to be done to fix it?" Dale would ask.

Dale would listen to the Lord. The Lord would give him the prophetic solution to the problem. When this happened, the people in the plant would ask, "How did you know what to do"? His response would be, "I prayed." After this happened several times, people would start to ask the question, "How did..."? They would stop and reply, "We know. You prayed." It was a testimony of how God has answers for the problems in the marketplace.

God intended for the entire world to enjoy His presence. When He created mankind, He put them into a garden that was to be extended into the entire world. The inhabitants of Earth would then experience the presence and goodness of the Lord. God's plan for man also included responsibility for the garden.

> The LORD God took the man and put him into the garden of Eden to cultivate it and keep it.
>
> Genesis 2:15

The word *cultivate* in the Hebrew language is *abad*. Some of the meanings of abad are to work, serve, or to plow. It also means to worship or to cause to worship. God intended for man to work the garden. Work before the Fall was not unpleasant. Man was to plow and bring increase into the garden. After man's Fall, the work became hard and difficult. Man needs the Lord to reveal solutions for tending Earth.

The world is looking for solutions to problems today. These solutions are needed in every mountain of culture. They are needed in the marketplace. As a marketplace person, you have access to the prophetic voice of the Lord from His Council Room. Your prophetic gift is not left in a church building on Sunday. You have access to your prophetic gift by entering God's Council Room every day of the week. Your solutions to today's problems will be used as a testimony to those who need a touch from the Lord. Don't leave your prophetic gift behind when you leave church on Sunday. Bring it into the marketplace and use it for the glory of the Lord!

William Wilberforce was a British politician and philanthropist. He lived in the late 1700s and was a leader of the movement to abolish slavery. His good friend, John Newton, authored the hymn, "Amazing Grace." They campaigned vigorously for Britain to use its influence to abolish slavery throughout the world. They were not a large group. Their group consisted of less than 20 people. The leaders were passionate about their faith, their causes and their commitment to them. After decades of work, the group saw the passing of the Slavery Abolition Act in 1833. Pooling resources and influence capital allowed for powerful results. Like Wilberforce and Newton, prophetic marketplace people are world changers. Be willing to dream big dreams from God. You have the solution to many of life's problems. Connect with others who have the same spiritual DNA. You were born for this moment in history. Don't miss your moment!

Practical Steps
1. What is Greek thinking?
2. What is a Biblical worldview or Hebraic thinking?
3. What Jewish tribe is described as having "an undivided heart"? What does that mean?
4. Describe a time in your life when you felt that a rug had been pulled out from under you. What did you do?
5. How do you receive a Word of Knowledge in the workplace?

CHAPTER 6

Prophesy to Nations and Territories

"Barbara, I need to know what to do!" I recognized the voice of the pastor on the call. He lives in a nation with few Christians. Most of the nation includes Hindus, Buddhists and Muslims along with indigenous spiritual beliefs. Yet, the pastor and his wife are making a great impact in the nation. They are reaching a young generation that is hungry for the Lord. They are gaining great favor with local and national government officials. The church members are embracing a kingdom mindset. The church members understand that God loves their nation. Prayer is a strong part of their lives.

The pastor continued talking and telling me what was happening in their nation. Comparatively, it is not a large nation, but a significant prophetic word had been released over the nation. Fear had gripped the hearts of many people. The word spoke of strong judgment and natural disaster that was going to happen in their small nation on a certain day. The people were already suffering from fear due to a natural disaster that had occurred a few months before. Now, they were told that another very powerful tragedy was going to happen due to their disobedience to the Lord.

I listened carefully to the story. I then asked a couple questions.

- *Who gave the prophetic word?*
- *Who are the prophets that judged the word before it was released?*

Intercessor Released Prophetic Word of Judgment for Nation

The pastor said the word came from an intercessor in a very influential church in the nation. After questioning the pastor, I discovered that the intercessor was a member of a church that does not believe in prophets for today. She was not a prophet but an intercessor. The pastor told me that he didn't think there were any recognized prophets in his nation to judge the prophetic word. The pastor for the influential church endorsed the word and had released it to the nation.

As I listened to the story, I found myself in the Council Room of the Lord. I needed to hear the wisdom of God for the situation. My pastor friend could not publicly come against the word. He did not have the same level of influence as the other pastor. His rejection of the word would create a problem for his church and the ministry. Yet, he could not embrace the word.

In the Council Room, I sensed a strategy from the Lord for the pastor. He needed to gather those pastors aligned with him. He didn't have authority over other churches. However, he had a responsibility to the pastors and people who were aligned with him. Let them know that he had talked with me as his apostolic accountability. I had evaluated the word. The conclusion was that the word of judgment for the nation came from an intercessor and not from a recognized prophet. The church and pastor she was aligned with did not endorse prophetic ministry for today. A strong word of judgment for a nation or territory should be evaluated by recognized prophets before being released publicly. That was not done. Therefore, the prophetic word was out of order. Prophetic protocol had not been observed for releasing a harsh word to the nation.

The pastor needed to tell the pastors aligned with him that the prophesied judgment would not happen! When the disaster did not occur, he would have proof, with the date written down, that he was told it would not happen. His pastors would respect him even more. They would realize that he is not an independent pastor. He is accountable. He does not embrace every word that is released. Words of judgment or disaster over a nation need to be carefully evaluated by recognized prophets.

The pastor followed through with the instructions that we had discussed. The pastors and churches aligned with him felt great relief. Fear lost its hold over them. The date for the disaster to occur came and went. Nothing happened. The churches aligned with my pastor friend recognized the value of proper protocol for releasing a word of judgment over a nation. They are teaching their people biblical principles for prophetic ministry.

How we need prophets and prophetic people to stand in the Council Room of the Lord to hear God's thoughts and His heart toward nations and territories! How we need to know the love of God for His nations! How we need to have Christians trained in prophetic ministry!

Prophetic Councils

I was a member of a group of nationally recognized prophets for several years. We gathered together a couple times each year. The purpose of the group was to hear what God was speaking to our nation. Various prophets would share what they sensed God saying from His Council Room. As each prophet spoke, the others would listen to the word. They would judge the word to sense if it was a correct word from the Lord. "Let two or three prophets speak; and let the others pass judgment" (1 Corinthians 14:29). After we had agreement on the words spoken by the prophets, the prophetic word was documented and released to the nation.

The prophetic council helped stop much of the wrong and often judgmental prophetic words that were being released in the nation. You always have a few weird, unstable people who give false prophecies. I remember seeing a huge billboard on top of a building in a very large city. The word said that the end of the world was coming in a few days. That did not happen! When prophetic people are educated in the word of God and taught proper biblical interpretation, people will stop listening to the false prophets.

Accessing God's Council Room to hear His heart and His thoughts for a nation is vital for strategies and revelation to touch nations. I love what my friend, Brother Jim Hodges, says about the necessity of entering that place with the Lord. We are able to see from His perspective and not from our own emotions or current events.

> We must see things from the throne's perspective before we can accurately see anything else. We must resist the tendency

to see events in history without seeing the view from the throne of God first. While secularists and humanists refuse to do this, the church must not fail to do it![8]

Prophetic Decrees to Redeem Nations

Nations are in God's heart! Nations had their beginning in Genesis 10. God put resources in each nation to bless them. Due to corruption, evil strongholds over those nations and false religions, many nations are experiencing poverty, murder, infirmity and all sorts of evil. These nations are living under curses rather than the blessings that the Lord planned for them.

In the same way that the Lord has a plan for redemption of individuals, nations can also be redeemed. Prophets and prophetic people can stand in the Council Room of the Lord to receive strategies, decrees and prophetic proclamations to help turn nations back to the blessings of the Lord. Ernest B. Gentile wrote about the Council of the Lord in one of his books.

> More than fifty years ago H. Wheeler Robinson wrote a journal article of particular insight. The prophet, he said, received his message from "the intimate council of the Lord." This thought is summarized in a later article. "The true prophets," Robinson wrote, "stood in the intimate council of the Lord where they received his word, his direction for the situation at hand...Admission to the

---

[8] Jim Hodges, *What in the World Is the Church To Do? The Seven Corporate Ministries of the Church* (Duncanville, TX: Federation of Ministers and Churches International), 29.

76

intimate council of the Lord meant special acquaintance with the will, purpose, and plans of the Eternal, which the prophet-observer, by virtue of his position, must declare to God's people. He was summoned by the Lord to announce the decisions of the council."[9]

Evil Decrees Overturned in Territories

Prophets, prophetic people and intercessors can stand in the Council Room of the Lord. They can hear the Lord's decrees for their territory. When they hear the thoughts of God for their territory, they can echo that sound back into Earth. That is how prophetic decrees are released. They are like echoes from the Council Room of the Lord. The person echoes or repeats the sound of the Lord from the Council Room back to Earth!

Decrees alter the spirit realm, so the will of the Lord is released into Earth. A decree is a law or judgment that is put in place. A decree can only be overturned by another decree. There are decrees of sickness, financial failure and corruption that are released over regions and nations. I sometimes hear pastors speak of their region as a "cemetery for pastors." In other words, churches and pastors are not able to be successful in that area. Those words are like decrees. Another decree needs to be released over the territory to break the power of that evil decree.

The Esther Company Arising

There comes a defining moment in history when God's

---

[9] Ernest B. Gentile, *Your Sons & Daughters Shall Prophesy* (Grand Rapids, MI: Chosen Books, 1999), 41.

people must arise from being pessimistic or paralyzed by apathy. In the Bible, Esther came to a defining moment in her life. Her nation, the Jewish people, was facing the threat of extermination. A decree had been released in the nation by the Persian king to destroy the Jewish people who were living in captivity.

Esther is a picture of a prophetic company that God is raising up today. She is totally controlled by Mordecai. Mordecai is a picture of the Holy Spirit. This radical Esther company is so in love with the Lord that she can't keep silent.

Like Esther of old, the Esther company is willing to take some risks. She is willing to step into the Council Room of the Lord by the power of the Holy Spirit. She is willing to converse, dialogue and strategize with the Lord for the salvation of her nation or territory. In that place, the Lord will ask a question. "What do you want?" When the earthly king asked Esther, she responded by telling him about the condition of her nation of Jews. The Persian king then extended his scepter of authority to Esther to issue a decree to overturn the evil decree against her people.

> Now you write to the Jews as you see fit, in the king's name, and seal it with the king's signet ring; for a decree which is written in the name of the king and sealed with the king's signet ring may not be revoked.
>
> Esther 8:8

An Esther company responds the way Esther in the Bible responded. She will converse with the Lord about the conditions of the nation. The Lord will extend His authority to the Esther company. The authority is for a purpose. The purpose is the saving of a nation or a territory. You will receive the authority to release the decree of the Lord as His spokesperson.

You have a prophetic decree from Heaven that can overturn ungodly decrees. King Jesus has given the Church an echo that must be released on Earth so that a nation can be saved. It is not enough to just get people saved and start new churches.

I live in an area that is often referred to as the most Christianized city in the United States. More people call themselves Christians in this city than any other city per capita in the United States. Yet, we still have crime, drugs, sex trafficking and all sorts of evil. Having more churches and more Christians does not transform a region or a nation. An Esther company needs to be part of the strategy in territorial or national transformation. Prophetic decrees are weapons that the Lord uses to defeat the enemy.

Decrees Can Be Songs

Decrees can be in the form of songs. A new song establishes you in the new place. A new song is a prophetic song. We see a prophetic decree being released in Exodus 15 at the crossing of the Red Sea. Moses and his people sang a song of thankfulness to the Lord. They also sang a prophetic decree from God's Council Room to the enemy that was occupying the land that God said belonged to the Israelites (Exodus 15:14-16). They prophesied fear, dread and terror to their enemies. These prophetic decrees often are ongoing until the fullness of God's will is completed on Earth.

The Israelites faced difficulties before possessing the promise they had decreed. They forgot their song of decrees when they entered into the wilderness. Without the echo—the song of decree—the wilderness causes you to lose your vision for the future. Without the ongoing prophetic decree, you will want to return to the last season and miss your destiny.

Later, when the spies were sent into the Promised Land, they witnessed the fulfillment of their prophetic decrees.

> When we heard it, our hearts melted and no courage remained in any man any longer because of you; for the Lord your God, He is God in heaven above and on earth beneath.
>
> Joshua 2:11

Rahab spoke the very words that had been sung over forty years before! Although the Israelites in the former generation forgot their prophetic song, the Lord did not forget. He held it in the atmosphere until a generation would rise and embrace the decree. The Joshua generation saw the fulfillment of a song of decree that had been released forty years prior.

Prophetic decrees were released over your territory or nation years ago. They are still in the atmosphere waiting for someone to embrace them. The will of God for your nation is waiting for you to pull down into Earth the promises for your generation. By faith, reach out and take hold of the former prophetic decrees for your territory. Prophesy them into your region. The will of God is waiting to be released on Earth!

As God's watchmen on Earth, we are not to stop releasing prophetic decrees until Earth looks like Heaven.

On your walls, O Jerusalem, I have appointed watchmen; all day and all night they will never keep silent. You who remind the LORD, take no rest for yourselves; and give Him no rest until He establishes and makes Jerusalem a praise in the earth.

Isaiah 62:6-7

The Lord is raising an Esther company on Earth today. She is neither male nor female. She is a triumphant Church that has been called to shift nations into their God-given destiny. Just as Esther in the Bible, you have been called to receive authority so you are able to fulfill your divine purpose.

You may not understand all that means for you. Probably Esther didn't understand all God intended for her life. However, as Esther walked forward in obedience to God, her life's plan unfolded. Your life's purpose will be the same way. The nations are waiting for you to respond to the call from God's Council Room. You are a member of the prophetic company that God is raising up today. We will talk about that company in the next chapter!

Practical Steps
1. What is a good protocol for judging words to be released over nations?
2. Who should release words of judgment over a nation?
3. What are some of the functions of prophetic councils?
4. How is a decree overturned?

5. What are some decrees in your nation or territory that need to be overturned?

CHAPTER 7

A Prophetic Company Arising

Dale and I were excited about our move to the Dallas, Texas area. We sensed a new beginning in our lives. I love new things. New clothes, new houses, almost anything new! I was sure that churches in a big city like Dallas would be operating in everything new that the Lord was doing. Since I was active in prophetic ministry, we looked for a church that embraced and released prophetic ministry.

How disappointing when we could not find what we were looking for! One of my favorite slogans is: *Somebody must do this. It might as well be me!* Since I could not find what I was looking for, I started prophetic training conferences at a hotel close to the airport. I wrote the syllabi for these training sessions and invited people from all over the nation. The attendees were so excited that someone would train and activate them in their Holy Spirit gifts.

A couple years later, I met Chuck Pierce. In 1994, we were asked to assist with an international gathering for leaders of intercessors in Seoul, Korea. The gathering was to develop strategy for AD 2000 and Beyond Movement.

The goal was to have a church for every people group in every nation by AD 2000 and Beyond.

Pioneering Prophetic Ministry for an Area

Chuck and I discovered that we both had a vision for prophetic ministry to breakthrough in our area. The Council Room strategy began to unfold. Every six months alternating between Dallas and Denton, we hosted prophetic conferences. Part of the strategy included praying at strategic places throughout the area. We also went onsite, prayed and held a conference in an area where the Jezebel spirit had a stronghold. The land required cleansing from bloodshed, religious unbelief and all sorts of defilement.

During these conferences, we activated prophetic people, prophetic intercessors and the worshippers. The worship team learned to access the Council Room of the Lord to hear the prophetic song for the conferences. Dancers were activated in prophetic dance. None of this occurred overnight. It took several years of persistent prayer, standing against cessationist mindsets throughout the area along with continual prophesying into God's destiny for the region.

Recently our church held a prophetic week. People were able to call the church and receive a prophetic word. The people in our church have been trained and activated in the prophetic. Many volunteered to answer calls and minister to people during the five days. Within that time, our staff and volunteers gave over 7,700 personal prophecies by phone including 301 in Spanish plus more than 1,275 through online chat. This number does not include the people who were not able to wait for up to an hour on the call to get connected to someone who would minister to them. What hunger in people for prophetic ministry!

Today, our area is known for the prophetic. The church and Global Spheres Center conferences are alive with a prophetic atmosphere each time people gather. Over 180 nations connect through various forms of communications including webcasting services, emails and postal services. A global prophetic company is alive throughout Earth! Many times, people think that this is merely an area that is open to the prophetic. They do not understand the long battle and continual listening to the Lord it took to shift this region. We had to access God's Council Room each step of the way. We had to hear His strategy for unlocking an area opposed to the prophetic. You can do the same thing in your area. *Someone must do this. It might as well be you!*

Valley of Dry Bones

Some areas are like the one Ezekiel found himself in. The Spirit of the Lord put him in a valley filled with dry bones. Ezekiel walked through the valley covered with dry human bones that were separated far from the temple of Jerusalem. He was in God's Council Room as they dialogued together about the future for that region.

> He said to me, "Son of man, can these bones live?" And I answered, "O Lord God, You know."
>
> Ezekiel 37:3

Often, we are like Ezekiel. The area we live in may seem hopeless. It may not have any visible evidence of life in the Spirit. These are times when a person must ascend to the Council Room of the Lord. The person must see from God's viewpoint and not from any human viewpoint.

> After these things I looked, and behold, a
> door standing open in heaven, and the
> first voice which I had heard, like *the sound*
> of a trumpet speaking with me, said,
> "Come up here, and I will show you what
> must take place after these things."
>
> Revelation 4:1

We are in a prophetic season of doors. God's Council
Room has an open door. He is inviting a company of
prophetic people to step through the door. In His
Council Room, He will show you what must take place.
You will inquire of the Lord, hear His instructions,
receive a new level of authority and go forth to prophesy
a hope and a future for your region.

Prophets Bring Recovery

God must have prophetic people who will be His agents
for recovery. This is a prophetic time to believe that what
was lost in your area can be recovered. God has always
had His people who could bring recovery where there
was loss.

Ezekiel had to prophesy to the dry bones. Where
there was death, the power of the prophetic words would
recover life! Ezekiel did not merely prophesy one time.
He listened to the Lord. He continued to prophesy and
call for the wind of God to blow on the dry bones.

I remember my early years of ministry. Many
times, I found myself speaking at meetings where people
were filled with apathy and discouragement. They seemed
to be half asleep. The worship time seemed more like
music at a funeral! I remember entering the Council

Room of the Lord to discover what to do. Should I get back in my car and drive home? No one seemed alive enough to even hear what I was prepared to speak. The people seemed ready to take a nap. Like Ezekiel of old, I heard the Lord speak. "Prophesy! Prophesy life!"

I knew the Lord had given me a key to unlock life where there was death and discouragement. Before speaking the message, I stepped forward and prophesied over several people. The place came alive! People seemed to wake up! They sat up in their chairs. They were hungry for more. The strategy that the Lord gave me so many years ago has been a key for breakthrough in many places. When people are hopeless and discouraged, prophecy can break the chains that are holding them bound. Prophecy is a life-giving spirit. It is stronger than the death in their hopes and visions. It is more powerful than discouragement. Prophecy gives hope for the future! "There is hope for your future," declares the Lord (Jeremiah 31:17).

Nehemiah Helps in Recovery

Nehemiah was a person that the Lord used to bring recovery. Nehemiah lived in a comfortable place as the cupbearer to the king. He could have chosen to stay in his comfort zone. However, he heard that God's people had returned from captivity to the city of Jerusalem. Although some progress had been made in restoring the city, much of the city was in devastation. The walls were still down. The gates were burned with fire. The enemy had access to God's people.

Nehemiah could no longer live in comfort while God's people needed recovery. He prayed and entered God's Council Room to receive favor to accomplish his task of recovery for God's people.

> Now it came about when I heard these
> words, I sat down and wept and mourned
> for days; and I was fasting and praying
> before the God of heaven.
>
> Nehemiah 1:4

Because of Nehemiah's meeting with the Lord, he gained favor and the approval of the king. Nehemiah was successful in his assignment due to the strategy and favor of the Lord.

> The wall was completed on the twenty-
> fifth of *the month* Elul, in fifty-two days.
> And it came about when all our enemies
> heard *of it*, and all the nations surrounding
> us saw *it*, they lost confidence; for they
> recognized that this work had been
> accomplished with the help of our God.
>
> Nehemiah 6:15-16

The prophetic company that the Lord is raising today functions the same way. They meet with the Lord. God gives them the prophetic word and strategy to bring recovery to individual lives, cities and regions.

Prophecy to Restore Destiny

Nehemiah was used to bring recovery to a devastated city. Often, we also see individual lives that are devastated. Mistakes were made in the past. Failures occurred. Guilt and remorse hang on year after year in the person's life.

I was speaking in a church years ago. I saw an older man sitting toward the middle of the church. I had never met him but knew the Lord wanted to speak a prophetic word to him. The word of the Lord came to me as I stood in His Council Room.

"Tell the man that I still need him," I heard the Lord say. He continued by saying, "I am ready to restore the ministry that was lost so long ago."

I spoke the words that I heard the Lord saying. The man bent over at his seat and began sobbing. After the meeting, he told me his story. He gave his heart to the Lord many years before. He loved the Lord so much that he wanted to tell everyone. When he would share about Jesus, people gave their hearts to the Lord. Healings, signs, wonders, miracles occurred.

When this started happening, the leadership of his church came to him. They told him that he had no authority to do such things. They demanded that he stop ministering to people. The man became so discouraged that he became an alcoholic. When this happened, the church dismissed him from membership. Later, they asked his wife and children to leave the church since the man was an alcoholic.

Now, his daughter and her husband were pastors of the church where I was speaking. He probably thought that the dream he had for ministry would be fulfilled through his daughter. He was too much of a sinner for God to ever use him again. He had messed up!

But God! The Lord knew the plans he had for this man. No religious system could stop God's plan! No alcoholism or other addiction could stop God's plan! No negative feelings of failure or defeat could stop God's plan for his life!

After the prophetic word, this man began ministering again after so many years of defeat. Later, he traveled to other nations. He held large meetings. People received Jesus as Lord of their lives. Signs, wonders and miracles were powerful in all his meetings! God restored years that had been stolen from this man's life.

> Then I will make up to you for the years that the swarming locust has eaten, the creeping locust, the stripping locust, and the gnawing locust.
>
> Joel 2:25

Restored Prophetic Vision

A prophetic word restored life where there was death to a vision! God is raising a company of prophetic people with vision. They have vision for the future. They dream the dreams of God. Peter spoke of this prophetic company by quoting the prophet Joel at Pentecost.

> "IT SHALL BE IN THE LAST DAYS," God says, "THAT I WILL POUR FORTH OF MY SPIRIT UPON ALL MANKIND; AND YOUR SONS AND YOUR DAUGHTERS SHALL PROPHESY, AND YOUR YOUNG MEN SHALL SEE VISIONS, AND YOUR OLD MEN SHALL DREAM DREAMS; EVEN UPON MY BONDSLAVES, BOTH MEN AND WOMEN, I WILL IN THOSE DAYS POUR FORTH OF MY SPIRIT and they shall prophesy."
>
> Acts 2:17-18

Vision gives hope for the future. Without prophetic vison people don't merely stand still. Like the man mentioned above, they go backwards. "Where there is no vision, the people are unrestrained" (Proverbs 29:18). People without prophetic vision can miss their destiny.

God's prophetic company is a company of seers. They see beyond the present and into the future that God has planned. Joshua and Caleb were people of vision. When the spies were sent into the Promised Land, most of the spies saw the giants. They saw the challenges and difficulties of possessing the Lord's promise. Joshua and Caleb were able to see beyond the giants and saw the prophetic promise of the Lord. God had prophesied for 400 years about the land they would soon possess. The time had arrived. The future was in front of them. Would they shrink back in fear or move forward in faith?

The older generation failed to make the right choice and move in faith that God would do what He said He would do. The Lord raised up a new generation to receive His promised blessings. The new generation under Joshua made the decision to crossover from where they were into God's prophetic promise.

Prophets and prophetic people face the same decisions today. God has a *now* time when He is ready to transition His people into a new prophetic season. He is calling a company of people to stand in His council, to see and hear His word and pay attention to what He is saying.

> But who has stood in the council of the Lord, that he should see and hear His word? Who has given heed to His word and listened?
> But if they had stood in My council, then they would have announced My words to My people, and would have turned them back from their evil way and from the evil

of their deeds.

Jeremiah 23:18, 22

Prophetic Generation Arising

God is bringing a powerful revelation to His Church at this time in history. He is bringing understanding of His plan for the Church in the earth. He is releasing His Church into her destiny as His representatives on Earth.

We must decree that His prophetic generation is here! This prophetic generation destroys demonic structures. It releases the spirit of wisdom and revelation. It brings breakthrough in every area of life. This prophetic call is available for all ages, every culture and race, and every economic group. This is the generation that shakes off shackles that have held people captive.

Apprenticeship and mentoring are often-neglected aspects of both family and church life in today's culture. Many families are dysfunctional, both in structure and relationships. We live in a disposable society. Products are used for our convenience and then thrown away. Too often relationships are treated the same way. If the relationship is no longer convenient or interferes with our own selfish desires, we simply discard it and seek a replacement. Our dysfunctional society affects the next generation. Relationship needs are overlooked as the demands of careers and high-paced living prevent the needed involvement of parents and other family members.

God is calling a prophetic company to arise and announce the word of the Lord to His people. You are part of that prophetic company! You are in a *now* season. You have been brought out of the power of darkness and entered the Kingdom of God. You now have access to God's heavenly council. The God of Glory longs to speak to you. He longs to have you see and hear His word. You have the privilege of giving heed to His word and announcing His word to Earth. Arise to your prophetic destiny! You were born for such a time as this!

Practical Steps

1. What are some steps that are necessary for a breakthrough in your area?
2. Who are some people that you can connect with to bring a breakthrough for prophetic ministry?
3. What are some areas of your life that need to be restored?
4. How does a person "see" the word of the Lord?
5. How do you overcome fear with faith for God's prophetic promises?

PRAYER

Father God,

Thank you for allowing me to live during this powerful prophetic time on Earth! You knew the best time for me to be alive. My desire is to fulfill everything You put in me that is necessary to accomplish your Kingdom purposes on Earth. I dedicate my life to You again. Use me for Your glory!

I declare that I am part of a privileged generation that is alive today. You are giving me access to your Heavenly Council. You are a good Father. I can stand in Your Council Room and converse with you. I believe You will speak to me. You will dialogue and strategize with me. You will reveal Your heart and Your plans for lives, territories and nations.

My spiritual ears are open to Your voice. Thank you for confirming Your call on my life. I close the door to my past. I reject intimidation, disappointments, failures and all negative feelings concerning who I am. I am Your child and loved by You. Therefore, I walk through the open door to my future.

I receive a new mantle of spiritual authority for my life. With that mantle, I now make decrees to change the future of lives, territories and nations.

- *I decree that I have a new mindset. I break the power of old religious mindsets. I embrace the operation of apostles, prophets and prophetic people that function today. I decree that I am part of today's prophetic generation that is arising. I will not be silent. I will prophesy the will of God into Earth!*

- *I listen to the dreams and visions You give to me. I believe You will give me interpretation. You will give me understanding on how to pray and decree Your will from these dreams and visions.*

- *I receive the operation of discerning of spirits in my life! I believe You will open my spiritual eyes and ears. I will discern Jezebel and false prophets that disguise themselves as your people. You will give me the wisdom to know what I need to do when I discern these evil spirits.*

- *I decree that you are revealing my spiritual parents, mothers and fathers, that will help me fulfill my destiny. You are also giving me prophetic mentors. Help me know the difference between my spiritual parents and my mentors. May I be a blessing to them and honor them with my life.*

- *I decree that You will go with me wherever I go on Earth. I will recognize You at work, in my neighborhood and in my daily activities. I reject the idea that You are only inside church buildings. I decree that my work and all activities will bring glory to Your Name.*

- *I decree that from this day forth, I am filled with vision for Your purposes in Earth! Like Joshua and Caleb, I see beyond the circumstances. I see the promises of the Lord. I am willing to war for those promises. Your voice from Your Council Room will empower me to decree and fulfill Your will.*

Thank you, Lord, for inviting me into Your Council Room. I accept Your invitation. May my life bring glory and honor to You!

PERSONAL REFLECTIONS

About the Author

Barbara Wentroble leads an apostolic network and a strategic alliance of visionary leaders globally. She is a strong apostolic leader, gifted with a powerful prophetic anointing. Ministering with cutting-edge teaching and revelation, a powerful breaker anointing is released. She teaches Schools of the Prophets and activates prophetic giftings in people. Giftings and anointings in ministers, business leaders and individuals are activated for the purpose of fulfilling their destiny.

Barbara conducts leadership conferences to emphasize releasing God's transformational power in cities and regions. She has been involved in the global prayer movement since the 1990s and travels around the world.

Recently Barbara launched the online course: *How to Become a High Level Prophetic Intercessor*. She is the author of ten books. These books include *The Council Room of the Lord: Accessing the Power of God; Prophetic Intercession; Praying With Authority; Removing the Veil of Deception; Fighting for Your Prophetic Promises, People of Destiny, and Empowered for Your Purpose.*

Barbara is founder and president of International Breakthrough Ministries (IbM) and Breakthrough Business Leaders (BBL). She and her husband Dale reside in Lantana, Texas. They are parents of three adult children and eight grandchildren.

Barbara's contact information:

Website: www.barbarawentroble.com

Email: info@barbarawentroble.com

Mailing Address: P.O. Box 109, Argyle, Texas 76226

Office Phone: 940-735-1005

Empowering Resources

Get Connected: Align with Barbara Wentroble
Phone: 940-735-1005
Email: info@barbarawentroble.com

Order Books, Products and Join Our Free Monthly Spiritual Growth Trainings:
Go to website: www.barbarawentroble.com
- Free Monthly Mentoring Calls
- Prayer Conference Calls
- Breakthrough Business Leaders gatherings:
  Local onsite meeting in Corinth, Texas or Facebook Live Broadcast

Complete travel and special events
schedule: www.barbarawentroble.com

How to Become a High Level Prophetic Intercessor.
Watch this 3-PART FREE VIDEO SERIES, online only.
- The Main TRAPS to Avoid...
- The Key SECRETS Intercessors should know...
- How to SHARPEN your Discernment...

Advanced Prophetic Intercessor
Online Training & Equipping for Individuals or Groups

Breakthrough Books
Prophetic Intercession
Unlocking Miracles and Releasing the Blessings

Praying with Authority
How to Release the Authority of Heaven

Fighting for Your Prophetic Promises
Receiving, Testing and Releasing Your Prophetic Word

Removing the Veil of Deception
How to Recognize Lying Signs, False Wonders, and Seducing Spirits

Empowered for Your Purpose
Keys to Unlock Your Future

Breakthrough Products
Breakthrough Anointing Oil

The Council Room of the Lord Series

This book, the second in the series, is to encourage believers to press into the Lord's Council Room to receive a Holy Spirit empowerment that is ushering in a powerful movement for the Kingdom of God. If you would like notification about future book releases in the series, please inform the office.

First Book in the Series

The Council Room of the Lord: Accessing the Power of God

93677906R00057

Made in the USA
Lexington, KY
17 July 2018